1 MONTH OF
FREE
READING

at

www.ForgottenBooks.com

By purchasing this book you are eligible for one month membership to ForgottenBooks.com, giving you unlimited access to our entire collection of over 1,000,000 titles via our web site and mobile apps.

To claim your free month visit:
www.forgottenbooks.com/free896451

ISBN 978-0-266-83460-1
PIBN 10896451

Historic, archived document

Do not assume content reflects current
scientific knowledge, policies, or practices.

DEPART

DE

Washington

With S

T

T
d
of

e
T
ea
year. A

C

UNITED STATES
DEPARTMENT of AGRICULTURE
DEPARTMENT CIRCULAR 400

Washington, D. C.   December, 1926

FOOT-AND-MOUTH DISEASE

With Special Reference to the Outbreaks in California, 1924, and Texas, 1924 and 1925 [1]

JOHN R. MOHLER,

Chief, Bureau of Animal Industry

CONTENTS

The appearance during 1924 of two outbreaks of foot-and-mouth disease in the United States was a cause for concern among livestock owners and seriously affected other industries. The following discussion sets forth, for the information of the public, the manner in which the outbreaks were met and overcome and includes also experiences likely to be of value in dealing with possible future outbreaks of the pestilence. Figure 1 shows the areas involved.

The more extensive of the outbreaks was discovered in California early in 1924, the other appearing in Texas in September of the same year. A recurrence of the latter took place in July, 1925.

THE CALIFORNIA OUTBREAK

The first intimation that foot-and-mouth disease had appeared in California occurred February 17, 1924, when J. J. Hogarty, a practi-

---

[1] The writer desires to express his appreciation of the splendid spirit of cooperation that was shown in the States where the outbreaks occurred, and to thank the governors of the States and State departments of agriculture, the livestock sanitary authorities, the Forest Service, the Bureau of Biological Survey, the Federal and State horticultural boards, the State fish and game commissions, Federal, State, county, and municipal officials, veterinary practitioners, livestock, dairy, and civic organizations, railroads, stockyards, and other business organizations, the press service, and the owners of livestock, especially those whose herds were sacrificed, for the valuable assistance which all rendered and which made it possible to eradicate the troublesome outbreaks of 1924 and 1925.

tioner at Oakland, who was also the county veterinarian, was called to see a small dairy herd of six cows at West Berkeley. The symptoms exhibited by these animals were such that he called Jacob Traum, of the University of California, in consultation. On February 18, while these men were at the farm, Doctor Hogarty received a telephone message from N. E. Clemens, a practitioner at Hayward, to the effect that the Shore Acres dairy herd—about 25 miles from Oakland and containing about 350 cattle—had several animals that showed suspicious symptoms.

Doctor Hogarty, with Doctors Traum and Hart, of the State university, visited the Shore Acres farm at once. As the lesions observed looked like those of foot-and-mouth disease, they took scrapings of infected tissues and inoculated two calves. Doctor Traum

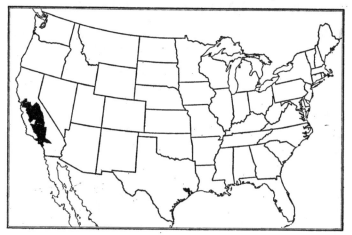

Fig. 1.—Distribution of infection in the 1924 and 1925 outbreaks of foot-and-mouth disease, involving 18 counties in two States. Other near-by counties and parts of counties were quarantined, but the infection did not develop in them

also took some of the material to the laboratory and inoculated two guinea pigs. The purpose of these tests was to determine definitely whether the suspected ailment was foot-and-mouth disease. The same evening Doctor Hogarty notified J. P. Iverson, chief of the State division of animal industry, who in turn informed Rudolph Snyder, in charge of field work, in California, for the Bureau of Animal Industry, United States Department of Agriculture. Early the following morning Doctor Snyder conferred with Doctors Traum and Hart at Berkeley. The two former, with R. E. Duckworth, of Iverson's force, proceeded to the Shore Acres farm and made another inspection of the herd. Lesions rather characteristic of foot-and-mouth disease were observed in several of the animals. Snyder immediately notified the Washington (D. C.) office of the Bureau of Animal Industry, reporting the findings described and stating the probability that the lesions were those of foot-and-mouth disease. Under telegraphed instructions from the bureau Snyder made further inoculations, including horses, hogs, and calves. Horses were inoculated to eliminate the possibility that the affection might be vesicular stomatitis, to which horses are very susceptible.

On the following day the first herd at West Berkeley was again examined. The animals in this herd were apparently recovering, and no typical lesions could be found.

The inoculated calves were normal on February 19, but on the 20th the temperature of both began to rise and one of them showed well-defined vesicles (blisters) about the size of a pea on the lower surface of the tongue. At this time Iverson telephoned G. H. Hecke, Director of Agriculture, at Sacramento, informing him concerning the situation. The former was instructed to establish all necessary temporary quarantines until the director could arrive in Oakland the next day and go over the situation on the ground. As a result the latter signed an emergency order on February 22 quarantining the movements of livestock in Alameda County.

The horses, upon inspection on February 22, proved to be normal, eliminating possibility of stomatitis and adding evidence of the presence of foot-and-mouth disease. Meanwhile the strange plague had been discovered in other herds of cattle and some infected hogs also were found. The veterinarians who had observed the affected herds and the inoculated animals unanimously agreed on the diagnosis of foot-and-mouth disease.

Within an hour after receipt of this information by telegraph, on February 23, the Secretary of Agriculture, acting under authority of law, issued an order placing under quarantine the counties of Alameda, Contra Costa, and Solano. The Bureau of Animal Industry also telegraphed veterinarians and other employees at widely separated stations, directing them to proceed immediately to Oakland. Practically all these employees had had experience in combating foot-and-mouth disease, and were selected under a plan worked out several years ago to occupy key positions in an emergency of this kind. So prompt was the response that many of these men were en route on transcontinental trains before the close of that day.

Meanwhile a series of other events and activities had transpired, largely of control and precautionary nature. Snyder had been authorized to use all his force in making inspections in suspected districts and was instructed to subordinate all other work to the emergency. The bureau's inspector in charge of virus-serum-control work at Berkeley, Calif., was warned of the danger of possible contamination of those products by foot-and-mouth disease and was directed to permit no new animals on the premises from any source until further notice. L. Enos Day, an experienced bureau pathologist, was ordered to California to assist in diagnosing the disease.

A supply of circular letters, previously prepared for such an emergency, was released. These letters described briefly the symptoms exhibited by affected animals and outlined the more important measures that should be taken to prevent spread of the infection and to accomplish its eradication. Bureau inspectors in charge of field work in Western States were notified by wire that an outbreak of foot-and-mouth disease had been confirmed in California and were directed to be on guard. Livestock sanitary officials, especially west of the Mississippi River, and officers in charge of animal-disease work in Canada and other foreign countries were also advised by wire of this outbreak.

Before a positive diagnosis of the disease had been made, the State authorities had closed the roads in the vicinity of the affected area and placed guards over infected premises and also summoned all available State forces. On February 24 and 28 additional bureau employees were ordered to Oakland. On February 25 the Federal quarantine was extended to cover the counties of Napa, Marin, Sonoma, San Mateo, Santa Clara, and San Joaquin.

The Government Printing Office gave excellent cooperation by printing the quarantine orders within a few hours and, also, in one night a special edition of the Farmers' Bulletin on foot-and-mouth disease. Thus was launched the fourth campaign against foot-and-mouth disease in the United States during the last 40 years, the latest previous one having occurred in 1914.

ORIGIN OF THE INFECTION

Federal regulations do not permit the importation, from countries where the disease is present, of animals, hides, and other products of animal origin liable to carry infection. The regulations require also that packing material, like hay or straw, from such countries must be either burned or disinfected under official supervision. That class of material is commonly used for packing china and fragile articles and the more common practice is to burn it. Livestock and their products, even from countries where there is no evidence of foot-and-mouth disease, receive careful veterinary supervision also.

Accordingly, in view of the fact that the infection gained entrance in spite of these precautions, two experienced inspectors were assigned to trace, if possible, the origin of the California outbreak. Their investigations covered such possibilities as: Feeding garbage from the Mare Island Navy Yard (near the scene of the outbreak); feeding coconut meal to cattle; salt used on imported hides, after it had been used by hog feeders following its removal from the hides; garbage from foreign ships, being washed ashore on the land of stock owners and eaten by their livestock.

The investigations included also the scrutiny of records containing lists of stores carried by ships suspected of carrying the infection, also thorough inquiry into the kinds and number of pet animals carried as mascots. All except the first of the suspected avenues of infection, when fully investigated, failed to explain the presence of the disease. But that one—the feeding of garbage from the Mare Island Navy Yard—resulted in a chain of evidence that accounted for both the appearance of the disease and its spread in Alameda and Contra Costa Counties, which, with Solano County, were the first counties affected. The investigators established the following facts: On December 10, 1923, lameness appeared among hogs (about 600 in number) owned and fed by I. B. Winslow, near Vallejo, Solano County. Winslow had a contract for removing the garbage from the Mare Island Navy Yard. Some of the hogs, according to the owner's description, were so lame and stiff that when aroused

they could get only to their knees. Six days later other hogs introduced on the same premises also became lame.

In the light of future developments the lameness was due to foot-and-mouth disease, though the owner did not suspect it at the time and he did not call a veterinarian. This hog feeder made shipments on December 3, 1923, and January 4, 1924, to a packing company at West Berkeley (Alameda County), Calif., the hogs being presumably infected on those dates. It is plausible to conclude that the disease was carried from that center to farms in Alameda and Contra Costa Counties through various agencies, such as trucks used to transport garbage, calves, and hogs into and through the yards, also by calf buyers going from farm to farm, and by laborers and milkers going from place to place in the vicinity. Several ships that had tied up at the Mare Island Navy Yard during November and December, 1923, had purchased supplies at foreign ports in the Orient, and the garbage contained a great deal of meat, but attempts to trace the introduction of infection to any one ship were unsuccessful.

EXTENT OF OUTBREAK

The work of suppressing the disease in the Oakland area, consisting of Alameda, Contra Costa, and Solano Counties, was pushed so vigorously and effectively that all infected herds were found by March 22, and four days later these and all exposed herds had been killed and buried. The policy of promptly slaughtering diseased herds, cleaning and disinfecting the premises, and remunerating owners for animals and property destroyed, had proved to be so successful in former outbreaks that it was adopted without hesitation for handling this one. With the exception of one recurrence of the disease on April 9, the three counties mentioned remained free from further infection.

The recurrence appeared in Pinole Canyon, Contra Costa County, and was due apparently to some stray cattle that had not been found in a very broken and wooded section of the district in which the disease had previously existed. This section was immediately and thoroughly combed by range riders and every animal found running at large in it was rounded up and slaughtered. The last diseased animals in that county were buried on May 15.

On March 22, however, when foot-and-mouth disease had been practically eradicated from the Oakland area, it was discovered in a large range herd of cattle in Merced County, one of the important stock-raising centers of the State. Thus, overnight, conditions underwent a complete change and the State and Federal forces faced a situation more alarming than at any time since the disease was discovered in California.

Another draft of Federal employees was rushed to this field and State forces were increased. But, in spite of everything that could be done, the infection spread quickly to a large number of herds in that county and to near-by herds in the counties of Madera, Mariposa, and Stanislaus. These counties constituting with Merced, what was known as the Merced area, were placed under Federal quarantine on March 24. In that area, eradication work was carried on under greater difficulties than had been encountered in any previous outbreak in the United States.

Among these difficulties were: (1) The spread of the disease to large herds of cattle and flocks of sheep in rough, inaccessible, and poorly fenced country suffering from the worst drought experienced in 30 years; (2) inability to obtain adequate trenching machinery quickly; and (3) delay in excavating on account of the character of the soil, which in many sections was underlaid with hardpan and rock. In spite of these obstacles, the campaign was waged with such energy and resourcefulness that control of the disease in that area was definitely established within six weeks.

The work of eradication in Merced County was scarcely begun when a dangerous situation developed in the southern part of California, infection being discovered in a packing establishment at Los Angeles on March 24, the day that the Merced area was placed under Federal quarantine. The infection in Los Angeles came from Merced County, having been carried by cattle shipped from there on or about March 19, which was before the time infection was discovered in that county.

The shipment showed no symptoms of the disease on arrival at Los Angeles, nor when part of the animals were slaughtered, on March 21, but lesions were discovered on the 24th, when the remainder, that meanwhile had been held in the packers' pens, were being slaughtered.

On the same day an affected hog was found as it was being unloaded into the yards of a slaughtering establishment at San Francisco. This animals was one of a lot shipped from Merced County. The pens at this plant and other packing establishments in the vicinity were at once closed for disinfection. Los Angeles and San Francisco Counties were placed under Federal quarantine on March 25.

On March 27, foot-and-mouth disease was discovered near Stockton, San Joaquin County. The infection in this instance also was traceable to a shipment from Merced County. San Joaquin County, however, had been under Federal quarantine since February 25. These instances show the extremely infectious nature of the disease and its habit of spreading with great rapidity unless checked by vigorous methods.

There was no spread of the disease in San Francisco, because of its prompt discovery and the immediate application of eradication measures. The infection was soon stamped out also in San Joaquin County, only seven herds being affected. But in Los Angeles County the situation had become very serious through the spread of infection to the holding pens of numerous slaughtering plants and large feed lots and to dairies in their vicinity. The stockyards and packing establishments were closed for cleaning and disinfection, which required several weeks. In spite of every precaution taken to prevent infection, one of the most valuable Holstein dairy herds in the United States fell a victim to the ravages of the disease and was slaughtered and buried the same as animals of plebeian breeding.

At Los Angeles, however, there existed **means** of salvaging livestock which had not contracted foot-and-mouth disease but were in grave danger of exposure. Several thousand animals of that kind were slaughtered and passed for food after having received the customary rigid ante-mortem and post-mortem inspections. As the animals if not slaughtered probably would have contracted the disease later, this disposal of them no doubt saved the State and Federal Governments about a quarter of a million dollars, that being approximately the amount their owners would have received as indemnities if it had become necessary to slaughter and bury the animals. Besides saving the animals for food, the reduced animal population in the danger zone lessened the opportunities for foot-and-mouth disease to spread.

Other counties in which outbreaks occurred were Kern on April 2, San Bernardino on April 21, Orange on May 2, Tulare on May 7, Tuolumne on May 9, and Fresno on May 12.

In all these counties except Tuolumne the outbreaks were limited and were stamped out quickly without involving any great number of animals. In Tuolumne County the situation was serious from the beginning, since the diseased herds were ranging in a mountainous, inaccessible country where it was practically impossible to dig trenches for the burial of infected animals. But a force of experienced men, assigned to that county, handled the outbreak so admirably that only 16 herds had contracted the infection up to May 21, a period of 12 days. The burial of herds was accomplished in some instances by slaughtering the stock in canyons and abandoned railroad cuts and then blasting the sides in to cover the carcasses.

After apparent freedom from infection for a period of 42 days, from May 21 to July 2, the disease again appeared, due probably to one or more infected stray animals in a large herd of cattle on their summer range in the Stanislaus National Forest of Tuolumne County. Within a few days infection was discovered in several other herds and the situation again became very serious. From July 2 to August 16 infection was discovered in 42 herds involving 6,917 cattle and 3,419 sheep. Since a 100 per cent round-up of the stock in that rugged country was impossible, final inspection of the stock could not be made until the animals were driven from their summer ranges by the advent of cold weather and heavy snows. The infection which occurred in the Stanislaus National Forest also spread to deer, creating still further complications. Briefly, the outbreak extended to 16 counties and, within six months, more than 100,000 animals were destroyed in bringing the pestilence under control. Besides the 16 counties each containing varying numbers of infected premises, 7 additional counties, in whole or in part, were under Federal quarantine, at different times during the outbreak, as "buffer" territory to control the disease.

ORGANIZATION OF FIELD FORCES

The legal and regulatory aspects in dealing with an outbreak of the disease came to the front at once. On February 21, the day after foot-and-mouth disease was strongly suspected, Doctor Iverson consulted the attorney general of California concerning quarantine laws. At the same time he notified the general freight agents of the three principal railroads in the State of the threatening danger. All agreed to enforce any quarantine that would be indicated by letter. The next day Alameda County was quarantined on order issued by Director Hecke.

Five days later formal State quarantine was established by governor's proclamation, and emergency rules and regulations were issued by the State Department of Agriculture. During this time the Federal quarantine orders had likewise been issued and were in effect.

At an evening meeting held February 22 all available bureau, State, university, county, and city employees were organized into one unit. Districts were laid out for farm-to-farm inspection, scouting work, investigating rumors, and tracing shipments. This organization rapidly gathered power as the Federal and State employees assigned to the work reported for duty.

No outbreak of foot-and-mouth disease was ever attacked more systematically nor with a better organized force of experienced men than was the California outbreak.

On February 23, the day the outbreak was announced, 14 outstanding and experienced bureau men were ordered to California and 16 more were ordered there on February 24. These 30 inspectors had been selected and listed since the previous outbreak on account of experience and other proved qualifications. · Headquarters were established at Oakland. G. H. Hecke, State director of agriculture, and J. P. Iverson, chief, division of animal industry, assumed charge of the eradication work for the State, and Rudolph Snyder was given supervision of the Federal forces.

The bureau decided that it was advisable also to give some of the younger and less experienced men an opportunity to see the disease and get experience in preparation for possible future outbreaks. Consequently, on March 20, 26 additional men were ordered to California from widely separated field stations. It was considered advisable to have available a surplus of men sufficient to handle any outbreaks that might appear in other parts of the State until additional assistance could be sent. Such outbreaks occurred the latter part of March.

By April 4 the Federal force numbered 110 men on the ground or en route. The number was increased until at one time there were 204 bureau men in California, exclusive of collaborators. The State also had a large force in the field.

On April 24, at the request of Governor Friend W. Richardson and Director of Agriculture G. H. Hecke, the United State Department of Agriculture took full charge of the campaign to eradicate foot-and-mouth disease. Headquarters were maintained at Sacramento, and U. G. Houck, of the Federal Bureau of Animal Industry, who was representing Secretary Wallace in this campaign in California, was placed in charge of both State and Federal forces.

METHOD OF ERADICATION

As already indicated, the method of eradicating foot-and-mouth disease was that of quarantine, slaughter, and disinfection. There are two other methods—(1) Immunization and (2) quarantine and disinfection—which are used abroad in attempting to control the ravages of the infection in countries where it is always present. But, for reasons set forth in Department Circular 325, which deals with foot-and-mouth disease with special reference to the outbreak

Fig. 2.—Driving cattle into trench for slaughter. Though drastic, this method of eradicating foot-and-mouth disease is effective and economical

Fig. 3.—One of the largest trenches prepared during the California outbreak. A steam shovel was used for excavating it. Note barrels of lime at left

of 1914, the only method now known that can be depended on for complete eradication in the United States or elsewhere is that of quarantine, slaughter, and disinfection.

The slaughter of infected and exposed herds was accomplished, in most cases, by driving the animals into a trench and shooting them there. A rifle of .25-20 caliber proved to be a very satisfactory weapon for the purpose. The handling and slaughter of condemned animals was performed in the most humane manner possible.

Following slaughter, all carcasses were thoroughly eviscerated and covered with quicklime. As a rule 1 barrel of lime was sufficient for every 6 to 8 cattle or 12 to 15 sheep or hogs. Details of methods are discussed in connection with problems encountered during outbreaks in the various counties.

QUARANTINE PROBLEMS

Early in the outbreak of foot-and-mouth disease in California, the livestock and other industries of the State began to feel the effect of embargoes and regulations imposed by other States against California products. Though the intent of the regulations was self-protection on the part of the States that established them, some were not only of doubtful value but were exceedingly burdensome to both shippers and transportation companies.

Thirty-six States issued embargoes against some or all of the following products originating in California: Livestock, meats, poultry, baby chicks, dairy products, hides and skins, wool, hay, straw, fruits, vegetables, nursery stock, canned goods, dried fruits, grain, biological products, emigrant movables, manure, bees, dogs, cats, pets, and automobile traffic.

Some counties in California placed embargoes against other counties, but the most serious regulations were those imposed by other States, especially neighboring ones. These placed serious burdens on the agricultural interests of California and on many branches of commerce, banks, railroads, and others both within and without that State, without affording increased protection to the livestock interests of the States concerned. Many of the embargoes were imposed without regard to how capable the products might be of carrying the infection, and applied equally to commodities originating in any part of the State, regardless of the distance from infected areas.

According to one report, a sporting-goods company had a shipment of clay pigeons turned back, and when the manager assured the responsible authorities that the birds were pigeons in name only and that they had just arrived from the East and had been reshipped in their original packing cases, he was told that the ban must stand because they were packed in straw. Losses suffered as a result of these drastic and in some instances unnecessary embargoes were many times greater than those caused by the enforcement of carefully considered Federal and State regulations, promulgated with the single purpose of controlling and eradicating the disease.

Moreover, the various regulations of different States changed with such rapidity that it was impossible for the employees of large railroad organizations to be fully posted, with the result that sometimes the carriers' agents accepted freight which later was not allowed to move through some State. This caused embarrassment and loss to shippers as well as to the railroad companies.

The following examples cited by the freight traffic manager of one of the principal railway systems illustrate this situation:

One State required the disinfecting of all cars containing commodities from California irrespective of their nature.

It was necessary to furnish disinfected cars to move cement from a plant 500 miles distant from point of infection.

One State's quarantine prohibited fruits and vegetables that were grown in California and placed an interpretation that rice was a vegetable, but if the rice were grown in China, Japan, or some other State it would be permissible to ship. It was impossible for railroad agents to distinguish between California-grown rice and rice grown in other States or countries.

Canned milk and canned meats were prohibited by one State, notwithstanding that these two commodities are classed as sterilized products.

Another quarantine prohibited dried fruit and beans that had not been in storage six months. This placed the burden on the railroad's agents to know the details of practically every man's business.

One quarantine prohibited garden and farm seeds unless they were last year's crop and in storage since harvested. It will be appreciated that a railroad agent can not keep track of all these details.

A car of railroad ties from a lumber mill in the extreme northern part of California was turned back on the border line of another State on account of the car's not being disinfected. This resulted in needless transportation and delayed the shipment materially.

A California State report referring to the same problem states in effect: The promulgation of embargoes covering the movements of not only animals but practically every agricultural product, by many States, soon became a matter of serious consideration. They were becoming more burdensome and stringent day by day and it soon became evident that organized efforts must be made to have unnecessary restrictions removed before the great field crops and the bulk of the fruit and vegetable crops were ready for marketing.

Following a series of conferences in Sacramento, a conference of Western States agricultural officials was held in Salt Lake City April 1, 1924. This conference culminated in the adoption of uniform State regulations by the States represented. The regulations provided for the shipments of nursery stock, fruits, and vegetables from California when packed with new paper or excelsior and accompanied by a certificate of the State or Federal Department of Agriculture certifying that the shipments originated on premises free from foot-and-mouth disease infection. It is estimated that close to a million separate shipments, many of which were car lots, were certified to under these provisions.

Both in connection with the general conduct of the field work and to relieve the presence of drastic quarantines imposed by other States, it became apparent to the director of agriculture of California during April that better organization of the forces could be obtained by unifying the command under the United States Bureau of Animal Industry. This action, it was believed, would instill more confidence into the situation on the part of other States. In compliance with this request, brought to Washington, D. C., by a committee of citizens representing the governor of California, Secretary of Agriculture Wallace placed U. G. Houck in charge of all foot-and-mouth disease eradication work in California April 24, 1924.

LEGAL AND FINANCIAL ASPECTS

As is customary, the expense of carrying on the work in California was shared equally by the State and the United States Department of Agriculture. In the beginning, however, the State had no specific fund with which to defray its share of this expense. The absence of any law specifically authorizing the slaughter of exposed animals tended further to complicate the situation unless funds could be provided to indemnify the owners of herds slaughtered.

No time was lost by these deficiencies, however, as Director Hecke, after conference with the governor and board of control, arranged with the bankers of California to advance sufficient funds and credit to cover the more pressing claims for indemnities. Later the bankers' advances and all other claims were liquidated through legislative appropriations. In the meantime money for the State's share of operating expenses was secured out of an emergency fund under supervision of the board of control. Thus the work proceeded without interruption and the State was enabled to cooperate with the bureau on a 50-50 basis.

CLEANING AND DISINFECTING

In eradicating foot-and-mouth disease one of the most important operations—vital for the success of the work—is the cleaning and disinfection of infected premises, of railroad cars, loading chutes, stock pens, and other equipment with which diseased animals may have come in contact. This work was directed and supervised at all times with the utmost care. First, the employees assigned to cleaning and disinfecting work assembled at an infected farm and worked together until the uniform methods of operation were well understood. The infected area was then mapped into districts and an experienced man assigned to supervise the work in each. When new men reported for duty they were detailed to work under trained supervisors until thoroughly familiar with all the details of the methods in practice.

As the infected area extended, new districts were organized, and as a rule the more experienced men were assigned to the new districts. In outlining the districts, the location of supply depots, the transport system, nature of roads, and the topography of the country were the determining factors. The districts, as organized for cleaning and disinfection, usually were larger than those established for inspection purposes.

Laborers were hired at prevailing local rates of pay. They worked in crews of from 12 to 24 men. One of the most competent men from each crew acted as foreman, and each crew worked under the direct supervision of an experienced bureau employee.

The standard equipment for a crew of 24 men was as follows:

10 manure forks (5 tine).	24 pairs of rubber boots.
6 scrapers (long handle).	48 suits of overalls.
6 ship scrapers.	4 pairs of rubber gloves.
6 heavy brooms.	8 flat shovels.
2 fiber push brooms.	2 scoop shovels.
1 crowbar.	6 hoes.
1 ax.	6 garden rakes.
2 milk cans (10 gallon).	2 picks.
1 pipe wrench (14 inch).	1 wrecking bar.
1 force pump.	1 hatchet.
100 feet ¾-inch pressure hose.	2 pails (galvanized, 12 quart).
2 rubber coats.	1 pair of pliers.
2 fumigating capes and equipment.	1 spray gun.

Two suits of overalls were provided for each member of the crews in order that one suit might be dipped, and, if necessary, sent to the laundry after being used. A hand-force pump was used for spraying small buildings; but power sprayers, rented or borrowed from city park commissioners or contractors, were used for large structures.

SUPPLY DEPOTS

Central supply depots were established at Oakland, Merced, and Los Angeles. In addition there were temporary depots throughout the infected area for the storage of equipment and supplies. All supply depots were kept well stocked with ample supplies of disinfectants and equipment. The principal disinfectants used were chloride of lime, cresol compound, and formalin. Equipment when not in use was returned to the supply depots and held for emergency use or distributed to other districts.

After a trial with four heavy Army trucks lent by the War Department, the bureau force found that light, commercial trucks were more economical to operate and were more satisfactory. They could move more rapidly and pass over all kinds of roads. One truck sometimes supplied two districts, but as a rule it was necessary to have a light truck with each crew. Besides distributing supplies and equipment, they were often used for transporting crews from place to place.

CLEANING PRIVATE PREMISES

Private premises classed as infected were cleaned and disinfected in the usual careful manner; all directly exposed premises were treated as infected. In the Oakland or bay district the cleaning and disinfecting operations were performed chiefly during March and April, which were rainy months, the corrals in many cases being very muddy. In such cases the manure was moved into piles with teams and scrapers. The surfaces of the piles, to a depth of about 18 inches, were treated to prevent danger from possible contact. Similarly, when fields had crops growing on them and the manure could not be spread on the ground and plowed under, it was disposed of by piling at some convenient place where it could be fenced away from livestock and held for about six months.

Some of the barnyards were floored with 2-inch planks or railroad ties. In such cases the floors were cleaned and then treated with a solution of chloride of lime. This solution generally was applied by dashing it on the floors from pails and then spreading it over the floors and into the joints by sweeping with push brooms.

Standing water in barnyards and pastures was treated with chloride of lime as were also all liquid-manure wells.

From about the middle of May until the end of the work, barnyards and corrals were very dry and the handling of manure presented a different problem. In the southern district the dairymen as a rule did not own farms but rented space for corrals and barn and purchased all their feed. The manure usually is sold to citrus-fruit growers. Under these conditions, when the premises were quarantined, there was no place for the manure except the corrals. In some cases the corrals were plowed and the manure turned under, but as a rule it was piled, treated with chloride of lime, and held until after the premises were released from quarantine.

Bunk houses on infected premises received special attention. They were well cleaned and then sprayed with cresol or formaldehyde solution. The clothing worn by milkers or attendants was usually dipped in formaldehyde solution and then laundered. Shoes were well cleaned and dipped, and the bedding was dipped and then hung in the sunshine; mattresses were sprayed and put out in the sunshine.

Pastures and ranges from which infected cattle were removed were not treated in any way except that all corrals, feed racks, water troughs, and like equipment were cleaned and disinfected, and all salt boxes were gathered and burned or disinfected.

GARBAGE-FEEDING PLANTS

Disposal of city garbage by feeding it to hogs is commonly practiced in California, and the hogs on eight of the large garbage-feeding farms in the State became infected. The method of procedure was to make an inspection of the infected premises, estimate the cost of cleaning and disinfecting, and the value of the property it would be necessary to destroy. If these estimates were about what the buildings could be purchased for, they were usually bought and burned. If it was possible to clean and disinfect them at less than the values of the buildings, they were cleaned and disinfected. Of six large outfits three were purchased and burned; the others were cleaned and disinfected.

PACKING ESTABLISHMENTS

Many of the large packing establishments in San Francisco, one in Berkeley, and all those in Los Angeles became involved. All were closed, the coolers emptied, and the entire premises were cleaned and disinfected in the usual manner. After a thorough cleaning, those rooms, where the odor would not be objectionable, were sprayed with cresol compound solution. The coolers, lard rooms, and storage rooms were sprayed with a 3 per cent solution of formalin and kept closed overnight, after which they were opened and aired out. The odor disappeared in a short time.

All small slaughterhouses in the quarantined area, known to be infected or exposed, were cleaned and disinfected as well as those in or near the quarantined area that were not known to have handled infected animals.

APPRAISAL OF PROPERTY DESTROYED

The property destroyed in cleaning and disinfecting premises usually consisted of contaminated grain, feed, grain bags, forage, hog troughs, and lumber torn out of buildings. All property destroyed was carefully itemized and recorded by the bureau employee who supervised the work. If the sum involved was small and the supervisor and owner could agree on the price, the necessary forms were signed at once and forwarded for payment. When a considerable amount was involved or the owner and supervisor could not agree, official appraisers were called in and the claim adjusted.

In some instances the owner of the cattle, feed, and equipment did not own the premises and it was necessary to render two or more accounts for property destroyed on one place. It was not found feasible to keep a detailed record of halters, ropes, and other small contaminated articles buried with the stock.

All property destroyed on private premises was appraised and vouchered for payment. In cleaning and disinfecting railroad stockyards, public stockyards, and feeding yards, packing houses, or other public or semipublic establishments, the bureau and State furnished experienced officials to supervise the work.

GUARD SYSTEM

The guard system inaugurated at the beginning of the campaign in the Oakland district worked well. The number of guards assigned to a ranch was determined by the size and nature of the premises to be guarded. Two guards were assigned to the smaller places, each man remaining on duty at the main entrance for 12 hours. Their duty was to prevent people from entering or leaving the place. In some cases it was necessary to place additional guards if there were other entrances to be guarded. In most of the infected areas a motor-cycle patrol was maintained to aid in the enforcement of the quarantine regulations. As a rule these guards were paid by the county and were under State or Federal supervision. When a place was cleaned and disinfected, the proper officer was notified and the guards were released.

DISINFECTING LARGE FEED YARDS

One mill company in California owns and operates a feed yard consisting of approximately 32 acres of concrete-paved pens. The feed consists principally of cottonseed hulls and concentrates, but no hay. Manure is allowed to accumulate in the pens during the entire feeding season, after which it is air-dried and sold to citrus-fruit growers. Foot-and-mouth disease developed among cattle in these yards early in April. At this time the manure was about 18 inches deep in the corrals and was valued at $150,000.

After the animals were removed the surface of the wet manure was covered with chloride of lime and turned under at once with gang plows drawn by tractors. About five days after the manure was plowed, it was disked, to mix the manure well with the disinfectant. The disking process was repeated about once a week until the manure was well dried.

The mangers and superstructures were cleaned and sprayed with 3 per cent cresol compound solution and the bottoms of the posts treated with crude oil. Sixty days after the premises were cleaned and disinfected, test animals were turned in on the manure and held there for 30 days. As the test animals remained free from disease at the end of the period the manure was released for sale.

An interesting side light on the cleaning and disinfecting work occurred in Los Angeles and shows the efficacy of the methods used. Ben Lewis and Don Lewis, father and son, worked as laborers on cleaning and disinfecting crews in an infected district from April 25 to June 26. During that period of about two months they lived at home, where they kept two cows. The cows were milked, fed, and attended to each day by these men while working with the crew. The cows remained free of the disease and continued so during the extent of the entire California outbreak.

THOROUGHNESS OF DISINFECTION

Altogether 702 premises were cleaned and disinfected in eradicating foot-and-mouth disease from California. Though animals belonging to 941 owners were kept on these premises, it is gratifying to report that in only two cases did the disease reappear. Both were in Merced County, not very far apart, and in both cases the disease appeared only in test animals that had been placed on the premises to determine the completeness of the eradication measures. In the first case, extensive investigations revealed no outside source by which the disease could have been caused. The reappearance was due necessarily to some lingering and persistent infection that survived cleaning and disinfecting operations. It is noteworthy that the test animals had been on the premises for more than 60 days before showing any signs of illness.

In the other case, in which recurrence of the disease appeared, investigation led to the conclusion that infected hay was responsible for the new flare-up. The old hay which was in the barn when the premises were disinfected was first fed by the owner about 10 days before the disease made its second appearance. The history of the case was as follows: First infection was discovered April 23, 1924; on April 25 the stock, consisting of 30 cattle and 21 hogs, was slaughtered and buried; disinfection was completed April 28; restocking with test animals occurred July 22; quarantine released October 24; infection again discovered April 5, 1925; cattle slaughtered and buried April 6 and cleaning and disinfecting begun the same day. These cases are described to show the persistence of the virus which causes foot-and-mouth disease. In the latter case the recurrence of the disease appeared nearly a year after the first outbreak and proved to be as clear-cut an experiment on the viability of the virus as if conducted and controlled under laboratory conditions.

In the remaining 700 premises on which the disease was present in 1924, no new outbreaks appeared following the work of the cleaning and disinfecting crews. This is a noteworthy record for thoroughness.

The procedure of releasing individual premises from Federal quarantine was simplified during 1924, compared with the method used in previous outbreaks. The new method, as prescribed in Amendment 22 to B. A. I. Order 287, enabled livestock owners to restock their premises promptly as soon as the inspectors authorized restocking. Instead of designating and describing the various small areas, which numbered several hundred, and issuing formal printed quarantine notices, as formerly, the new document authorized field headquarters to issue notices of removal of quarantine restrictions. This action simplified and hastened the lifting of quarantine as soon as the test periods expired, thereby permitting dairymen and other livestock owners to resume their business promptly.

TRACING, CLEANING, AND DISINFECTING RAILROAD CARS

In view of the extensive movement of railroad cars, the disinfection of those carrying diseased animals or otherwise exposed to the disease was highly important. At the outset of the campaign to eradicate foot-and-mouth disease, a bureau inspector interviewed operating and accounting officials of the railroads, including electric lines, operating within the State. These officials assured their full cooperation in the tracing, cleaning, and disinfecting of cars.

Then, immediately after the receipt of telegrams from the Washington office showing areas quarantined in various parts of the State, it was the practice to telephone all railroads operating in the quarantined area, requesting a list of all cars carrying livestock during a period of possible exposure to the disease. On receipt of this information the first step was to locate all cars for cleaning and disinfection. The lists received from the railroads showed origin, date, consignor, car number, contents, consignee, destination, and sometimes other special information. With these records it was possible to send an inspector direct to the premises containing the animals that had been shipped. This plan facilitated prompt inspections of such stock.

Every movement of cars which carried animals later found to have been diseased, though not showing visible symptoms at the time, was carefully traced. Lay inspectors stationed at various points in the State supervised the cleaning and disinfection of cars and made their reports to a central office. Large numbers of all types of cars, including box cars for commercial purposes and poultry cars, as well as stock cars, were disinfected under Federal supervision. This action was necessary, since States bordering on California required all such cars, whether loaded or empty, to bear cards showing that the cars had been cleaned and disinfected under Federal supervision. The railroads did not confine themselves to disinfecting only those cars coming under Federal regulations, but disinfected all stock cars on their lines, whether they had been in federally quarantined areas or not, and continued to disinfect them after each shipment.

The importance of car tracing may be illustrated by a few actual shipments. Three cars which carried infected cattle from Merced, Calif., on March 18, into the Union Stock Yards, Los Angeles, were located and disinfected there on March 27, before they were again loaded with livestock; of course, it was not known at the time of shipment that the cattle were diseased. Likewise a car that carried infected hogs from Merced to San Francisco was run down and disinfected under Federal supervision before it carried any more livestock.

The magnitude of cleaning and disinfecting work is seldom realized by persons not engaged in this activity. One railroad company arranged for the disinfection of 1,000 livestock cars to be used in transporting fruit to canneries of the State, the fruit being carried in boxes. Disinfectants used included chloride of lime, 2 per cent formalin solution, 3 per cent solution of cresol compound, and other permitted disinfectants, according to the nature of the commodity to be carried. Chloride of lime was the cheapest of the disinfectants, but formalin was employed in disinfecting box and refrigerator cars used to carry fruits, vegetables, and other articles that absorb odor. During the active period of suppressing foot-and-mouth disease (February 28 to July 19) more than 21,000 cars were cleaned and disinfected under Federal supervision. This branch of the work included also investigations of shipments by water. Several shipments of alfalfa hay carried in steamships loaded at San Francisco and consigned to eastern points via the Panama Canal were traced back to the point where the hay had been cut, baled, and stored to determine whether it had been handled in infected areas.

ERADICATING THE DISEASE AMONG DEER

On July 12, 1924, a new and very serious development, owing to the discovery of infection among deer, occurred in the work of eradicating foot-and-mouth disease. A local cattleman found a dead deer on the Niagara range of the Stanislaus National Forest which aroused his suspicions because of lesions on the feet and mouth. Their appearance so closely resembled those he had seen in his cattle that had been slaughtered for foot-and-mouth disease on that range a few days before that he brought the head and feet into camp for veterinary inspection. A careful examination by two qualified inspectors indicated strongly that the deer had contracted foot-and-mouth disease. Snyder confirmed the diagnosis, which was verified also by Houck and the writer.

A serious situation already existed in the Stanislaus National Forest owing to the discovery of the disease in cattle on that range 10 days before. The probability of infection among other deer, coupled with existing ravages of the disease in livestock in the wooded wilds of the public domain, presented the most serious situation of its kind ever encountered in this country. Never in our history had foot-and-mouth disease invaded a region so rough and inaccessible and never had it attacked deer or other wild animals.

The task of eradicating so virulent a disease from wild deer on the open range was further complicated by public sentiment against the destruction of such captivating creatures. Deer are protected by the game laws, the State fish and game commission being their guardian in California, and it was necessary to obtain the consent of the commission before any steps of eradication could be taken. In addition, it became evident at once that knowledge as to certain habits of the deer in this section, especially as to their drift or tendency to wander, was lacking. Information received along these lines in the beginning differed greatly. Before the extent of the disease among deer could be determined, a campaign of investigation was necessary. Accordingly, a conference was called at Sacramento on July 16. At this meeting the State department of agriculture was represented by G. H. Hecke, the fish and game commission by J. S. Hunter, the United States Bureau of Biological Survey by Charles Poole, and the veterinary work of the United States Department of Agriculture by Doctor Houck. Several other officials and business men also were present.

At this conference it was agreed that Poole, as the cooperating representative of both the State and Federal Biological Survey in California, would head an investigating party, including representatives of the Biological Survey and the State fish and game commission, which would begin operations at once. The chief aims of this expedition were to determine the local habits of the deer, decide on proper, efficient, and humane methods of taking specimens, and ascertain the extent of the disease.

The investigation, which began July 20 and ended August 13, developed the following facts: (1) A definite diagnosis of foot-and-mouth disease in deer; (2) a decision that strychnine poisoning was the best means of taking specimens, especially where shooting might scatter exposed and infected deer; (3) the unanimous opinion of the party that the deer were traveling or drifting within the immediate area instead of migrating to other localities. The last piece of information was encouraging, as it was evident at this time that the disease was confined to deer on the Niagara range and was not spreading to deer on other ranges. The fish and game commission therefore authorized on August 25 the taking of deer on the Niagara range. Infection appeared in deer, however, on the Clavey and later on the adjoining ranges. As a consequence, on September 3, the fish and game commission agreed to deer operations wherever deemed necessary by the foot-and-mouth eradicating forces.

About this time an antagonistic spirit was shown by a small group of persons in Sonora and vicinity who were opposed to killing the deer. On September 8 this antagonism culminated in the leader's proposal to take a mob up to the hills and drive out the foot-and-mouth workers. To avoid violence Poole called out his men until the threatened uprising subsided. Following a public meeting in Sonora, September 12, at which officials and business men interested in the complete eradication of the disease were present, sufficient calm was established to permit the work to go on. However, the antagonistic elements never ceased in their efforts to hamper the work. Another impediment to the deer work was the fact that about 40,000 cattle and sheep were ranging in the Stanislaus National Forest, completely surrounding the infected area, and their safety would be threatened if commotion within the infected area scattered the deer. It was evident after studying the local habits of the deer that the best prospects of eliminating the disease among them was the destruction of as many deer as possible after they had become settled on their winter ranges.

It did not seem possible that the thousands of cattle and sheep grazing on the ranges of the Stanislaus National Forest could be saved, in view of the presence of infected-deer areas. However, the effort was considered worth while. Through the cooperation of the United States Forest Service, all permittees using the Stanislaus forest were ordered to remove all their livestock under the supervision of Federal and State inspectors by October 1, which was a month earlier than usual. Almost to a man they cooperated whole-heartedly, and the livestock was successfully removed from the forest after receiving very careful inspection. All were permitted to go to their home ranches except a small drove which on October 9 was found to have contracted foot-and-mouth disease on the way home. Two separate outbreaks occurred in deer, corresponding to those of cattle—on the Niagara and Clavey ranges. The extent of infection in those areas, while the deer were grazing, with little movement, on the summer ranges did not exceed that of a township each; but as the deer were driven down by the storms to their winter range they carried the disease with them. The spread of infection in deer within the infected areas was rather rapid and increased as they grouped more closely on their wintering grounds.

In conducting the campaign, one force of men was engaged principally in scouting outside the infected area to keep an accurate check on the spread of infection. A corps of expert diagnosticians, assigned to deer work, observed closely the nature of the lesions— whether new or old—thus establishing fairly definitely the history of the cases. The remainder of the force devoted their efforts to exterminating the deer in the infected area. This area was surrounded by camps, usually tents, each accommodating from 2 to 10 hunters. Each camp had a definite hunting ground with a foreman in charge. He kept a daily record of each hunter's work and rendered a weekly report to the Sonora office. In addition to having the necessary cooking and sleeping facilities, these camps usually had telephone service. Eradication measures included both poisoning with strychnine and shooting, depending on the conditions.

In investigating the extent of the disease at the beginning, it was found that the Niagara range was well supplied with salt logs, all of which were frequented by deer. These salt logs were the logical and in fact the only practical places to bait the deer. All salt logs throughout and around the Niagara district were first baited with several varieties of feed until it was determined which appealed to them most. They accepted different baits in a small way, but they preferred salt almost to the entire exclusion of other things. After the bait was taken freely, the salt was dosed with strychnine. In the use of poison and salt it should be borne in mind that sick deer are rarely killed in that manner, since they seldom eat, and the sick animals that were taken had been taken alive and killed.

In poisoning with strychnine, powdered alkaloid strychnine is mixed with ordinary table salt in the proportions of 1 part of strychnine to 3 parts of salt. It is placed, in amounts of 1 to 2 heaping tablespoonfuls, in piles, on salt logs which have been used for many seasons in salting cattle. The entire deer population had been accustomed to coming to the salt logs for salt and they thus took the poisoned salt readily, except in winter. At that season deer take little salt and poisoning was less effective. However, it continued to be a weapon in the infected area, though hunting with guns was practiced on the outer zone with the view of discouraging lateral drift as well as to obtain specimens. Outside the known infected area scouting trips were frequently made to check up the possible spread of infection. When such spread was disclosed, the camps were immediately moved in that sector to include the new territory within the area of intensive operation. Three trap corrals and one-half mile of drift fence were built near Lumsden bridge to keep a check on the condition of the deer which migrated from the mountains to the foothills.

Hunters were required to bring the feet, tongue, or other portion of deer carcasses showing any abnormality to camp, where facilities were maintained to hold specimens, awaiting diagnosis. The veterinarians assigned to making the diagnoses visited designated camps, examined the specimens, determined the status of the disease, and supervised the destruction of the specimens. They also consulted with the foreman of each camp as to the area covered by the hunters, and various other matters pertaining to the work. All reports from camp foremen and veterinarians were assembled at the Sonora office and a complete report submitted to Sacramento headquarters. At the peak of the work the force consisted of more than 200 persons.

The argument was advanced that the deer were being killed by bears and that the dead deer found probably were perishing in this manner. Though it is known to be almost impossible for a bear to capture deer, it seemed advisable to show by actual evidence that the bears which were invading the range in considerable numbers were not feeding on fresh meat, which would be the case if they were killing the deer. Accordingly some bears were obtained by poisoning and the stomach contents examined. The result showed deer heart and liver that contained maggots almost fully developed, proving that the deer on which the bear had fed probably had been dead three or four days. This observation, together with the fact that an abnormal number of bears was in evidence and more coming in each day, seemed to establish the fact that they were gathering on an area which afforded a large supply of putrid meat on which to feed.

Investigation of the deer situation showed also that foot-and-mouth disease was present both in a virulent type that kills the animal in a short time and in a less virulent form which enables the animal to recover and become normal in health so far as outward appearances show. The poisoned deer apparently met death in a reasonably humane way since, when found, they had traveled but a short distance from the place the poison was taken.

Success in eradicating the disease from the deer in the Stanislaus forest was indicated early in January, 1925. The last active infection among deer was found June 10, 1925. Twelve months later, June 10, 1926, all Federal quarantines in California were revoked after continued inspections showed that no virus remained in the previously infected territory.

Following is a brief summary of the progress of foot-and-mouth eradication among deer for the period November 19, 1924, to July 4, 1925, during which active eradication measures were in progress:

Number of camps maintained _____ 10 to 42
Number of hunters_____ 39 to 204
Number of deer taken weekly_____ 118 to 1.452
Total number of deer exterminated_____ [2] 20, 819
Per cent of infection, including healed lesions, observed weekly____ 8.9 to 37.25

Per cent of active infection, 24 to 0 per cent, as eradication work proceeded.

As a precautionary measure, the Forest Service, at the suggestion of the bureau, closed Stanislaus National Forest to grazing during 1925.

Notwithstanding that, through the methods of eradication employed, there was a consistently uniform decrease in the infection among deer, the opposition from some citizens of Tuolumne County to the eradication work was so pronounced in April, 1925, and also there was such great fear among the business men in some sections of the State over the possibility of the infection spreading from the deer, with the resultant repetition of the 1924 outbreak with its radical embargoes, that at the request of the State authorities the Secretary of Agriculture sent a personal representative to California to act in an advisory capacity to the various cooperating agencies. R. A.

---

[2] During the entire campaign 22,214 deer were destroyed, of which 2,279 showed lesions of foot-and-mouth disease.

Oakley, of the Federal Horticultural Board, was selected for this mission and he remained in California from May, 1925, to the following September, during which time he rendered valuable services, especially along the lines of personal relations.

TYPES OF LESIONS OBSERVED

In outbreaks of foot-and-mouth disease in the United States before 1924, lesions observed in cattle were rather uniform. Few of the animals presented lesions that were not typical of the disease. But in the California outbreak, several herds of cattle were encountered in which the lesions were of an unusual nature, making diagnosis difficult. In order to bring out this point more clearly, it is necessary to point out the more common symptoms and lesions in typical cases.

Frequently a veterinarian's attention is not called to the ailing animal until after the earlier symptoms and excessive salivation and vesicle (blister) formation are well established. This is especially true, on account of the rapid development of the disease, if the cattle are out on a large range or in a field where they are not seen several times a day by the owner or attendants. Excessive salivation usually begins with the first eruption of vesicles anywhere within the mouth cavity, regardless of their location or size.

The early symptoms in typical cases of foot-and-mouth disease include elevation of temperature ranging from 103° to 105° F. or even higher. The temperature is frequently preceded by rigors, their severity depending on the elevation of temperature. High temperatures are more frequently seen in fat, heavy cattle. Other constitutional symptoms are dullness, general depression, lack of appetite, suspended rumination, and a tucked-up appearance of the abdomen. The muzzle is dry; the mouth cavity is at first dry and clammy and the patient frequently grinds its teeth. Constipation is commonly present. If the animals are at pasture they usually separate themselves from the others, and if forced to walk, show tenderness, stiffness, or even marked lameness. In dairy cows there is an abrupt suppression of the milk flow. The symptoms described depend in degree on the severity of the disease.

MOUTH LESIONS

During the first 24 hours of the onset of the disease, vesicles begin to form, and with their formation occurs a profuse flow of saliva which is frothy at first and accumulates around the lips from which it falls in large drops. Later the saliva becomes thick and assumes a ropy character and is often mixed with shreds of epithelium (surface membranes), and dribbles from the mouth in large, stringy masses, often extending from the mouth to the ground. The muscles about the mouth are tense and the mouth remains closed most of the time. Occasionally, when it is opened, large quantities of thick saliva escape.

In the early state the mouth lesions can be felt as small, hard, elevated bodies about the size of hempseed. The most common place for them is the inner surface of the upper and lower lips. They also occur frequently on the tip and margin of the tongue and on the dental pad. These elevated bodies quickly enlarge to form vesicles varying in size from that of a pea to a walnut or even larger. Several small vesicles frequently coalesce and form larger ones; in other cases, as on the tongue, they become from 1½ to 2 inches in diameter without coalescence. The vesicles are yellowish white and contain a light, straw-colored, limpid fluid which gradually becomes turbid. Beginning with the formation of vesicles, the animal produces a characteristic smacking sound, apparently caused by sucking the tongue against the hard palate. As soon as the vesicles have broken, the smacking increases for a day or so and then gradually diminishes. After the vesicles have ruptured, the loose epithelium is shed, leaving a red, denuded area with a definite margin which contains shreds of loose epithelium clinging to it. The denuded areas correspond in size and shape to the ruptured vesicles. Soon after the formation of vesicles in the mouth, they may appear on other parts of the body, as the feet, muzzle, in the nostrils, and on the udder and teats.

FOOT LESIONS

In cattle the formation of vesicles on the feet may occur at the same time as those of the mouth, but they usually appear later. In lightweight dairy and stock cattle the location of vesicles on the feet is commonly at the place where the two toes join and around the coronary band. The vesicles occur also at the base of the dewclaw and in such cases the dewclaw usually is shed.

Generally all four feet are affected, but in lightweight cattle one or more may escape infection. The first indications of infection of the feet are heat, tenderness, and slight swelling around the coronary band. The vesicles range in size from one-fourth to one-half inch or more in diameter. Sometimes several small ones may coalesce and form a vesicle an inch or more in diameter; this happens more frequently in connection with the plantar cushion and around the coronary band than between the toes. Frequently in cattle when several vesicles form along the coronary band they coalesce and the skin separates from the horny structure and becomes loosened from the sensitive laminæ. In the course of healing, this crack remains between the newly formed horn and the old wall and can be seen for many weeks or until the new horn has grown down to the point of the toe and is worn off. Separation of the plantar cushion may occur in cattle of all ages and weight.

The process of repair in typical cases is rapid. This is particularly true of lesions in the mouth and on the muzzle. In these locations healing is well advanced in from two to three weeks provided no complications are present.

Foot-and-mouth disease in hogs, in the California outbreak, pursued a course typical of that of former outbreaks in the United States.

LESIONS IN SHEEP

Two bands of sheep—one in Mariposa County, consisting of 5,614, and the other in Madera County, of about 6,124—received special study with respect to the nature of the lesions. In both these bands approximately 15 per cent of the sheep were affected. In one band the infection was introduced by the sheep grazing over a pasture where infected cattle had grazed; in the other the source of infection was not satisfactorily traced. In both instances the vesicles were similar to those found in cattle, only much smaller. In many instances only one or two feet were involved; when the forefeet were affected the sheep walked on their knees.

LESIONS RESEMBLING THOSE OF FOOT-AND-MOUTH DISEASE

The diseases which resemble and may be confused with foot-and-mouth disease are: Vesicular stomatitis, mycotic stomatitis, necrotic stomatitis, and infection and injuries to the mouth by awns of various grains and grasses.

Vesicular stomatitis is a contagious, eruptive disease of cattle, horses, asses, and mules. It is characterized by the formation of vesicles and by erosion in the mouth and on the tongue. When cattle are afflicted with this disease it may be readily confused with foot-and-mouth disease. . The distinguishing points, however, are as follows: Hogs, sheep, and goats exposed to vesicular stomatitis under natural conditions have not contracted the malady, but they are very susceptible to foot-and-mouth disease. On the other hand, horses, asses, and mules have not been observed to contract foot-and-mouth disease in any of the outbreaks in this country but are very susceptible to vesicular stomatitis. An animal affected with the latter disease, when free in a pasture, usually stands with the back arched and head extended. If made to move it does so freely and rarely shows signs of tenderness or stiffness. Although there is a flow of ropy saliva, it is not so thick and tenacious as in foot-and-mouth disease. In vesicular stomatitis of the cattle examined in the field, the formation of vesicles is usually confined to the mouth cavity, but occasionally the feet and also the teats will show lesions. In foot-and-mouth disease all the vesicles which form in the mouth do so as a single crop within 12 or 14 hours after the first ones appear. In vesicular stomatitis this is not the case, as the eruption continues for a number of days and may extend over a period of about 6 to 8 days. Consequently, healed areas, denuded areas, and unbroken vesicles are found in the mouth at the same time; healing is taking place at one point while new vesicles are forming at another.

In foot-and-mouth disease, practically 100 per cent of the cattle in a herd become affected, whereas in vesicular stomatitis about 60 per cent is the greatest proportion to be afflicted. However, in the inoculation of calves and horses, we have a certain final test. If both these species of animals develop characteristic blisters in from 24 to 96 hours after inoculation, the diagnosis of vesicular stomatitis is warranted. On the other hand, if the calves show typical blisters in 24 to 72 hours and the horses remain unaffected, foot-and-mouth disease is indicated. Care should be taken, however, in the selection of test animals. Mistakes have been made by selecting healthy animals from infected herds and although apparently normal when inoculated, they nevertheless had previously been infected with either one or the other of these diseases and were therefore temporarily immune. Of course, under such conditions they gave negative results.

When test animals are necessary, assurance should be obtained that they are from herds where the disease under investigation had not occurred.

Mycotic stomatitis is a contagious disease of cattle, caused by the irritating effect of a fungus or mold on the mucous membrane of the mouth and occasionally on the thin skin at the juncture of the clefts of the toes. Sometimes the teats and other tender parts of the body are affected. The disease usually appears after the first rains in the fall of a year following a dry summer.

During the fall of 1924 mycotic stomatitis appeared on several premises in Tuolumne, Stanislaus, and Merced Counties. The disease was confined principally to adult cows which were poor in flesh and had calves at their sides. Steers and stock cattle which were in a thrifty, growing condition were not affected. ' Only from 1 to 5 per cent of the cows in the herds became affected; calves nursing infected mothers did not contract the disease. In one instance hogs that fed in the same lot with two affected cows and drank from a watering trough supplied by the overflow from the cattle trough did not contract the disease. In another instance cattle, hogs, sheep, and goats fed in a field with an infected cow did not contract the disease. In all cases animals affected with mycotic stomatitis recovered in from 8 to 14 days.

The first symptoms were salivation, tucked-up appearance of the abdomen, loss of appetite, partial or complete suspension of rumination, and diarrhea. There was a profuse discharge from the eyes and nostrils, which at first was thin and watery but soon became thick and purulent. The muzzles of affected animals became very dry, reddish brown in color, and leathery in appearance. In from two to three days the dried, leathery, superficial skin cracked loose at the margin of the hair and peeled off, leaving a raw, painful, granular surface having a pitted appearance which in some cases extended into the nostrils. The membranes lining the mouth and lips were congested. The free margin of the lower lip and dental pad and also the floor of the mouth for about an inch just behind the incisor teeth were highly inflamed.

In a short time a membrane formed which was greenish yellow in color and gave off a foul odor. The necrotic tissue soon sloughed away, leaving a denuded, red, granular surface. The external surface of the teats peeled off, leaving a raw surface. In some cases the legs were swollen, the swelling extending from the hoof to the dewclaw and even to the knee or hock. In none of the cases were vesicles observed on the feet. From the symptoms and other conditions outlined, it will be seen that mycotic stomatitis differs from foot-and-mouth disease in the nature of the lesions but chiefly in the fact that the former is not transmitted, by contact or otherwise, to hogs, sheep, or goats. Foot-and-mouth disease is easily transmitted to these animals.

During the California outbreak of foot-and-mouth disease nearly all the cases of mycotic stomatitis encountered were in the quarantined area. Consequently it was very important to distinguish between the two.

Necrotic stomatitis is a cattle disease that destroys portions of the lining membrane of the mouth cavity and is followed by the formation of yellowish, cheesy patches. In this disease vesicles do not form. It affects only a small proportion of the herd and therefore is readily distinguished from foot-and-mouth disease.

AWNS OF GRAINS AND GRASSES

The awns of certain grains and grasses sometimes cause an inflamed condition of the mouths of domestic animals. (Fig. 4.) The grains most responsible are barley, rye, and bearded wheat, when the straw of these grains is fed. Grasses that frequently cause sore mouths are wild rye, foxtail, and pin grass. These grasses are sometimes found mixed with the hay or other fodder. The barbs of the awns irritate tender portions of the mouth, producing painful, ul-

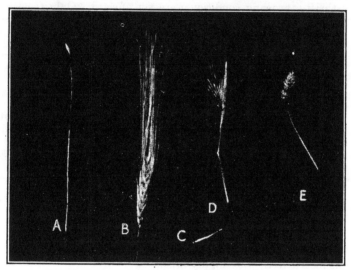

FIG. 4.—Common causes of mouth drool that may produce lesions resembling foot-and-mouth disease: A, Barley beard; B, barley head; C, spikelet; D, bristly foxtail; E, chicalote

cerated areas and excessive salivation. These conditions are readily distinguished from foot-and-mouth disease, as the offending agent can be found on careful examination of the mouth. (Fig. 5.)

LESIONS IN DEER

Because the deer in the forest were very wild and remained hidden from view in the brush, none were caught during the very early stages of foot-and-mouth disease. Though many affected deer were later obtained for study, only a small proportion showed acute lesions; with these exceptions all cases were of from four weeks' to two months' or more standing, when the vesicles had ruptured and repair had begun.

In the most recent cases observed, the vesicles were typical of foot-and-mouth disease, occurring in the same locations as noted in cattle. Their size, however, was considerably smaller, as would be expected, and rarely exceeded the size of a pea or bean. After rupturing, the margins of the resulting erosions were rather regular and depressed, appearing in every way like those of foot-and-mouth disease in cattle after the vesicles had ruptured, except that they were smaller and on the tongue presented a neater, punched-out appearance. As a result of the coalescence of several blisters at the tip of the tongue, the mucous membrane became denuded for one-half to three-fourths of an inch, leaving a raw surface. These erosions on the tongue seemed to heal readily, but on the dental pad and

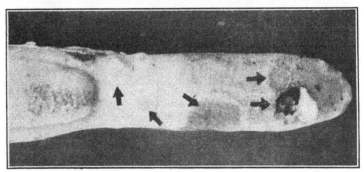

FIG. 5.—Comparison of lesions caused by foxtail (above) and by foot-and-mouth disease (below). In wounds caused by foxtail the irritating spikelets usually can be found by careful examination. This type of wound differs materially from typical lesions of foot-and-mouth disease shown in lower picture; arrows point to several unbroken vesicles and to one, near the tip, that has just ruptured

around the inside of the lips ulcerations were noted, as in cattle. All four feet were not infrequently affected. In some cases there was complete separation of the walls of the hoofs at the coronary band as well as of the plantar cushion, and in these instances the foot lesions were like those so frequently observed in hogs.

In all the older cases, the mouth lesions had healed. The lesions in the feet consisted of separation of the hoof wall at the coronary band and new hoof was being produced above. In older cases this resulted in the formation of marked ridges like those observed on the hoofs of a foundered horse. In practically every case all four feet were affected in this manner. Though, as stated, the febrile stage of foot-and-mouth disease in deer was not observed, the lesions in the acute, subacute, and chronic cases conformed with those of cattle.

TREATMENT WITH CHLORINE GAS

The use of chlorine gas by the medical profession for treating colds and certain other infections suggested to a number of persons, including Army officials, the possible effectiveness of the same gas for protecting livestock against infection by foot-and-mouth disease. Acting on the request of the Secretary of Agriculture, the Bureau of Animal Industry gave the gas treatment a trial under conditions where it would not be a source of danger or interfere with the work of eradicating the disease by the slaughter method. The sole object was to test the effectiveness of chlorine gas as a preventive rather than as a cure.

A total of four herds received the chlorine-gas treatment, two of which had been exposed to foot-and-mouth disease. The corrals in which the two exposed herds had been confined were of barbed wire, one of the corrals cornering the corral of a herd that had been infected. The diseased herd was buried on May 5, and disinfection of the premises was completed May 7. Gas treatment of the two exposed herds was begun May 5. The animals of both herds were driven into a barn closed as completely as possible, and an attempt was made to maintain a concentration of 500 cubic centimeters of gas per 1,000 cubic feet of space. A 2-hour exposure was given, and the treatment was repeated the following day. On the third day symptoms of foot-and-mouth disease developed in the animals of one herd, but as the two had been so closely associated both herds were slaughtered.

Two other herds were were likewise gassed, but the treatment was finally discontinued since there was no definite history of exposure, and it was believed that nothing definite could be determined by treating herds that were not known to have been exposed. One of these herds was given a 2-hour treatment daily for 4 days, after which the treatment was given on alternate days for a period of 1½ hours and continued for 10 days more, making the total duration of treatment 2 weeks. The temperature of the barn ranged from 78° to 108° F. during the treatment. The fourth and last herd treated was gassed for a period of 16 days under favorable conditions. Neither of these herds became affected with foot-and-mouth disease, but there was no direct exposure to infected stock. It was found difficult to maintain a uniform distribution of the gas, as it tended to settle to the barn floor unless agitated by men moving about in the barn and fanning with squares of pasteboard.

Because of the impracticability of its application under the conditions encountered, it was not considered safe to trust to the doubtful value of this gas in other dairy localities with near-by herds; in the case of isolated beef herds facilities for gassing were lacking. The few tests are presented as a matter of record and possible interest, but the results are considered lacking in scientific value. The Bureau of Animal Industry has pointed out on frequent occasions the dangers of performing detailed research and experiments with foot-and-mouth disease in the United States. The bureau, however, arranged during 1924 for such work to be performed abroad by three qualified scientists, one of whom is an employee of the bureau. This committee began its studies and research early in 1925, with headquarters at Strasbourg, France.

ADMINISTRATIVE DISTRICTS, REPORTS

This report already has outlined briefly how, early in the campaign, foot-and-mouth disease yielded to the eradication measures in the Oakland area, but later broke out elsewhere. In suppressing these outbreaks in various localities experience has shown the desirability of field offices at strategic points, each reporting, of course, to central headquarters.

Following were the principal field offices and administrative districts established during the California outbreak:

Sacramento.—State headquarters of Federal and State forces.

Oakland.—Field headquarters for bay district, including Alameda, Contra Costa, San Francisco, and Solano Counties; early in the campaign Oakland was the general headquarters for the Federal force.

Merced.—Field headquarters for district, including Merced, Mariposa, Madera, and Stanislaus Counties.

Los Angeles.—Field headquarters for district, including Los Angeles, San Bernardino, and Orange Counties.

Fresno.—Field headquarters for Fresno County.

Porterville.—Field headquarters for Tulare County.

Sonora.—Field headquarters for Tuolumne County.

Though conducting their work in substantially the same manner the different field offices encountered special problems. Those of chief value for the future deal with the manner in which the disease made its appearance and the manner in which the inspecting forces coped with different situations. Table 1 is a statistical summary of the California outbreak, and following are brief discussions based on reports of supervising inspectors.

TABLE 1.—*Statistical summary of California outbreak of foot-and-mouth disease, 1924*

County	Herds	Owners	Premises	Cattle	Hogs	Sheep	Goats	Total	Appraised value	Burial expenses	Property destroyed	Outbreak diagnosed	Disinfection completed
Alameda[1]	22			1,461	4,331	1	4	5,797	$181,284.62		$13,062.35	Feb. 22	Apr. 3
Contra Costa	253	71	10	6,728	3,281	42	160	10,211	427,190.07		2,454.31	Feb. 22	Mar. 17
Fresno	71			1,029	27	0	44	1,100	38,261.50	$4,837.28	94.12	May 12	May 30
Kern	7			176	4	0	1	181	7,788.90		485.31	Apr. 2	Apr. 12
Los Angeles	280	287	241	12,411	8,090	14	431	20,953	1,713,374.04		6,283.57	Mar. 24	Aug. 28
Madera	30	30	12	4,544	118	8,667	14	13,343	289,310.75	6,930.04	25.00	Apr. 25	May 26
Mariposa	14	14	12	1,220	340	5,614	14	7,174	85,716.00		55.00	Apr. 6	June 9
Orange	130	127	702	18,701	2,098	10,605	50	31,454	989,398.65	[1] 41,266.23	1,713.98	Mar. 22[2]	June 24[4]
San Bernardino	23	23	23	481	4	0	12	497	56,508.50		23.34	May 2	May 28
San Francisco	1	1	2	2	1,508	0	0	1,510	15,854.00		None.	Apr. 21	May 2
San Joaquin	1			0	19	0	0	19	276.50		None.	Mar. 24	May
Solano	7			333	0	0	7	340	17,625.00		242.92	Mar. 27	Apr.
Stanislaus	5		3	528	518	0	64	1,110	53,271.30		981.84	Feb. 22	Apr. 22
	3	9	8	146	117	15	0		6,470.50		6.00	Apr. 12	Mar. 23
Tulare	9	69	33	577	387	0	0	964	31,307.50		127.34	May 7	Apr. 26
	85			10,454	293	3,424	604	14,775	372,653.42	36,629.03	25.00	May 9	Oct. 16
Total	941			58,791	21,195	28,382	1,391	[3] 109,766	4,286,291.25	36,629.03	[4] 25,560.08		

[1] Includes Mariposa County.
[2] On September 26, 1924, and April 5, 1925, small outbreaks recurred in Merced County on two premises which had been cleaned and disinfected. Both were promptly suppressed.
[3] Not including 22,214 deer destroyed in Stanislaus National Forest.
[4] Not including $100 expended in San Mateo County.

MERCED DISTRICT

Foot-and-mouth disease was first found in Merced County on a ranch about 6 miles north of Merced. The finding of infection started with working the cattle on another ranch owned by the same company about 8 miles to the east on March 13 to 15. About 250 fat cows and 241 cows with veal calves were cut out of the range-pasture herds and on March 16 were driven along the public highway to headquarters on the first ranch mentioned, where the company conducts local slaughter.

On the following day the ranch foreman noticed that several cattle in the herd were lame. The county veterinarian and also a local veterinarian were called in and pronounced the lameness due to traveling over the gravel road the previous day. On March 21, the foreman, who had seen foot-and-mouth disease in the Philippines, noticed that several cattle were sick, showing lameness and drooling. He noticed also that several hogs that were feeding on offal from cattle of the herd were very lame, apparently trying "to walk on their knees." Not satisfied with the previous diagnosis he notified the Oakland office of his suspicion. G. A. Pfaffman, of the State force, was the first to respond to the call and he diagnosed foot-and-mouth disease. L. E. Day, of the Federal force, and Doctor Boyd, of the State force, arrived in the evening of the same day and on the following morning they confirmed Doctor Pfaffman's diagnosis and the ranch was quarantined immediately. On March 22 inspections were made of remaining cattle on the ranch from which the cattle came and the disease was found throughout the range of approximately 25,000 acres. The same day about three-fourths of the 85 hogs fed on the offal of the cattle showed pronounced symptoms of the disease. Many of them could scarcely rise after lying down and others were walking on their knees.

Plans were made at once for placing a force of veterinarians and assistants in the county to eradicate the disease, and at the same time ranch employees were put to work moving the cattle on both the ranches involved to "inside" pastures for isolation so far as possible. Preliminary inspection and survey work on adjoining ranches revealed a wide spread of infection and by April 1 approximately 8,000 cattle were found to be affected.

Inspections of cattle were made every day for at least 10 days on premises adjoining infected premises. These inspections were extended to all livestock on all suspected premises at least once a week for 30 days. In the badly infected sections the inspections were made for a period of 60 days from last infection. Repeated canvass inspections were made of premises within a radius of from 10 to 15 miles of infection. District supervisors received prompt reports of suspicious and infected cases, confirmed diagnoses of infected herds, and arranged for prompt quarantine of premises, location and size of trench, and dates for appraisals of herds. The organization included a State quarantine division with a supervisor in charge who arranged for closing roads when necessary. He also assigned guards to premises, these men working on 12-hour shifts, keeping constant guard until all livestock were slaughtered, and the premises cleaned and disinfected.

The organization included also an appraising crew, slaughtering crew, disinfecting division, permit division and a supply division. Branch headquarters were established in the adjoining counties— Mariposa, Madera, and Stanislaus—when infection appeared there, but the work was directed from Merced by personal conferences and long-distance telephone.

In several instances guards were placed inside of large ranches for patrolling the premises, keeping trespassers off, and killing coyotes and stray animals.

ROAD DIPS

The county officials in all four counties—Merced, Mariposa, Madera, and Stanislaus—were active in the early part of the cam-

FIG. 6.—The use of road dips for disinfecting the wheels and running gear of vehicles caused considerable annoyance to travelers and was of doubtful necessity except at the entrances of quarantined premises. The shoes of travelers also were disinfected, as illustrated. Certain counties enforced such operations for a time, but on the recommendation of bureau and State veterinary officials gradually discontinued them

paign placing troughs or road dips at various points on the highway. (Fig. 6.) The troughs were filled from 4 to 6 inches deep with a sheep-dip solution through which automobiles were required to pass.

These dips proved to be very objectionable and created the impression among the less-informed citizens that they were thoroughly disinfected, resulting in travel to premises where livestock was kept. As soon as county funds became exhausted, the road dips were discontinued. It is suspected that in many instances travelers evaded road dips and road guards by driving around them and through adjacent premises.

SUPERVISION OF SLAUGHTERHOUSES

When the disease was first found in Merced County, two local slaughterhouses were found to have slaughtered infected cattle.

The houses were placed under State quarantine and all unsold meats were traced, condemned, and destroyed. Meat boxes and premises were cleaned and disinfected, and both establishments were held under quarantine and tested with test animals in the usual manner. The operations of other slaughtering establishments were suspended for 60 days, after which livestock was moved to them only by permit and for immediate slaughter.

RANGE-RIDER LINES ESTABLISHED

When the disease was found in Merced County, the problem of preventing range cattle from drifting from the lower foothills of Mariposa County into the mountains was recognized as very important. Seven range riders were employed as bureau agents and assigned to patrol a designated line, thus maintaining a vacated area free from cattle along the line. The line riders were closely supervised by a bureau employee, but in spite of all these efforts three ranches above the line became infected. Another range-rider line was maintained along the San Joaquin River, restricting travel and movement of livestock across the river to the large range on the west side of it. In a range area, lines of the kind described are practically essential in controlling the disease even though the method is not always 100 per cent effective.

From the beginning of the campaign in the four counties mentioned, severe drought caused a shortage of feed and added to difficulties in conducting the work. When it became necessary to move cattle and sheep to save them from starvation, these movements were strictly supervised. Certain safe trails were designated and repeated inspections were made of the stock while moving and afterwards. A number of herds of cattle and bands of sheep were moved in this manner into the national forests for grazing. The stock was held for reinspection at the forest line for several days after leaving the home range. Final inspections also were made before turning the animals loose on the forest range. Forest Service employees gave excellent cooperation by furnishing full information on range conditions and advising cattle owners that bureau requirements covering foot-and-mouth control superseded Forest Service requirements. Forest Service employees also rendered valuable assistance by arranging with cattle owners for repeated inspections of livestock on the forest ranges.

SPECIAL PROBLEMS

In addition to the drought conditions already described as affecting the range cattle, other difficulties in the dairy sections complicated the problem of disease eradication. The Merced River section near Snelling was a badly infected district consisting mostly of dairies scattered over larger ranches. Several dairies often used one entrance and the pasture fences between the dairies were poorly kept. Cattle from several dairies sometimes grazed together, thus causing direct contact of various herds. Practically all dairies were operated by Portuguese, some of whom seemed unable to understand quarantine requirements. The sheep owners of the region grazed their sheep about 2,000 to a band, paid little attention to fences, and usually watered at one place. Consequently the infection developed in all the bands using the same pasture or watering place.

Another problem involved the irrigation system of the region. One of the main irrigation canals extended through several infected ranches. Infected cattle had watered in the canal and, to avoid possible spread of infection to the alfalfa-and-dairy section adjoining the cattle ranches, the water was cut off from the canal. This action caused considerable criticism, but after about 30 days from date of quarantine the water was again turned into the canal and the irrigation company gave the water a heavy charge of chlorine. No later infection was traceable to the irrigation water.

TRENCHES

The slaughtering of the large herds on the two ranches first affected was carried out as fast as six machine shovels could prepare trenches. These trenches ranged from 14 to 18 feet wide, 7 to 9 feet deep, and from 300 to 500 feet long. Building corrals and chutes for driving the cattle into trenches required a great deal of time and labor. Consequently several trenches were made leading from one point in order to use the same pen and chute. The machine crews worked day and night on 12-hour shifts. When herds had to be driven across highways to the trenches the trail across the highways was disinfected with chloride of lime immediately afterwards. On account of rocks and hardpan, trenches were sometimes made by selecting natural hollows or dry ravines. Hand laborers and teams were used for shaping the sides and filling in end walls. Trench space was made in a few hours' time in this manner and the cattle were killed more promptly. But refilling required more time because it involved digging hard soil on the sides for covering and working drain ditches around the trench.

SUPERVISING CREAMERIES AND DAIRY PRODUCTS

Within 24 hours after the first case of foot-and-mouth disease was found in Merced County, 25 deputized inspectors were stationed in Merced, Madera, and Stanislaus Counties. The movement of all dairy products was made only under permit. Trucks gathering milk and cream received permits to do so only after they had been properly washed and disinfected under supervision. The permit designated the origin of route or location of creamery, the truck number, route to be followed while collecting the product, point of destination for Pasteurization, and date and time of leaving the plant.

All milk and cream originating in infected territory was collected at the roadside. When the product arrived at the plant cans were first dipped in a solution of chloride of lime, 1 pound to 3 gallons of water. All empty containers were then washed and sterilized by steam and dried before being returned to patrons. Clean cans were placed on clean floors only, the floors being disinfected with chloride-of-lime solution. The truck drivers disinfected their shoes and changed overalls after each trip.

When, after Pasteurization, cream was moved from Merced County to other counties, the driver received a permit which entitled him to move from Merced County to point of destination on the highway only and without stopping en route except at proper disinfecting stations. The permit designated the number of cans, contents, name of creamery, license number of truck, and the date and time of leaving the plant where the cream had been Pasteurized. It also indicated whether sample bottles were being carried; and if so, that the contents had been properly disinfected by the use of a preservative. In this manner each truck that carried any dairy product was first checked into the infected area and then checked out and was at all times under control.

Pasteurization temperatures of all milk and cream were checked daily. Raw milk was sold only under special permit, a daily inspection of the herd being required. The manufacture of cheese was prohibited unless the type of cheese made was from Pasteurized milk or from milk heated to a higher degree than that of Pasteurization.

RESTOCKING

In view of the large range pastures infected and also late infection developing 30 days or more after the first infection found in the vicinity, it was arranged to withhold restocking the premises with test animals until 90 days after slaughter of the infected herds. The same requirement was applied to the Merced River valley premises, where small lakes and swamps rendered conditions unfavorable for sunshine to dry out infected places. Other small premises were permitted to restock with test animals 60 days after cleaning and disinfection.

MOVEMENT OF HAY AND WOOL

Movements of hay within the quarantined area were not permitted until after inspection of the livestock on the premises, and the delivery of hay was restricted to avoid exposure to other livestock. No hay was allowed to move from quarantined premises until after the premises were tested with livestock. All hides and pelts moved from the quarantined area of this district were dipped under supervision, using 3 per cent cresol solution or 1 pound of chlorinated lime to 3 gallons of water. Wool from the quarantined area was moved by permit direct to the scouring plant at Stockton, Calif., after spraying sacks with a disinfectant. Wool from quarantined premises was fumigated on the premises, sacks were sprayed with disinfectant and shipped direct to the scouring plant.

The infection was probably carried to the first ranches at the beginning of the outbreak in Merced County by a calf buyer who left Oakland to go to Merced on February 15, the week before the disease was known to be in California. On March 17 a local veterinarian visited the ranch, cattle being sick at the time, and immediately drove to another ranch and treated a sick cow; six days later this herd developed the disease. The further spread of infection was due probably to driving cattle over the same trail used by diseased cattle, and in two instances perhaps by roving dogs.

OUTBREAK IN MADERA COUNTY

On April 25, 1924, foot-and-mouth disease was discovered in Madera County. The infection appeared simultaneously on a sheep ranch and on an adjoining cattle-and-hog ranch. On the former ranch there were 6,124 sheep, which were divided into three bands; but only one band of about 2,000 head showed infection. This band watered in a hole near the river, which was intersected by the fence dividing the two ranches. It is probable that this water hole was the medium through which the infection spread from one ranch to the other. Further investigations revealed several possible channels of infection leading both to the sheep ranch and to the stock ranch, so that it is difficult to determine which was infected first. The sources include: A visit from a sheepman, one band of whose sheep was later found infected; Mexican laborers who had visited relatives and friends in the Merced district, which was infected; and woodchoppers who came back and forth daily from the vicinity of Merced to the stock ranch until a short time before the infection was discovered.

As the soil on the two ranches was sandy and easily dug, the trenches were made with teams and scrapers. The manner of disinfecting such an outfit after use is of considerable interest. A trenching outfit consisted of 5 men, 30 mules, 2 horses, 6 scrapers, 2 plows, 1 watering trough, 1 feed wagon, 1 large truck wagon, harnesses, ropes, bedding outfits, and personal belongings. The place of disinfection was on the roadside at the ranch entrance; the weather was fair and warm. Traffic over the road had been restricted. The drivers were first divested of their clothing and supplied with overalls and jumpers. Their clothing was dipped in a 1-to-1,000 solution of bichloride of mercury and hung on the fence to dry.

The mules were then disinfected. One mule at a time was unhitched, twitched, and harness removed. The guards stationed at this post sprayed each piece of harness. One driver held the twitch, another cleaned the frogs of the hoofs with a hoof knife, while two others sponged the animal completely with a 3 per cent solution of cresol, and each foot was submerged in the solution. Some of the mules were very fractious and had to be "hog-tied." As the disinfection of each animal was completed it was led across the line into free territory.

The rest of the equipment was sprayed with cresol solution with the exception of the bed rolls, which were sprayed with 10 per cent formaldehyde solution and rolled up damp. After the mules and equipment were disinfected, the drivers were divested of their overalls and jumpers, bathed completely with a 1-to-2,000 bichloride solution, reinvested with their own clothes, fumigated with formaldehyde gas, and allowed to proceed.

The force for suppressing the outbreak of foot-and-mouth disease in Madera County was divided into three divisions: The permit force, quarantine force, and the eradicating force. This county was under "closed quarantine"; consequently any movement of cattle had to be accompanied with a permit after inspection. The permit force was in charge of a veterinarian of the State who was familiar with the territory, people, and local conditions; his assistants were composed mostly of veterinarians of the State and county.

The quarantine force was headed by a State highway patrolman, who was detailed to assist in the emergency of disease eradication. He was assisted by a local stockman, employed by the State, who was in charge of the various guards on the premises and highways and the enforcement of quarantine laws and regulations.

The duties of the eradicating force consisted of house-to-house inspections, supervising the digging of trenches, range riding, and the destruction of diseased herds. The territory surrounding each point of infection was divided into areas of a size so that one inspector could make inspections of the stock at least once every two days, and of stock adjoining the infection once every day. These areas were marked off on a map and were bounded by some geographical marking, such as a road, township line, or river.

Officials and residents of Madera County cooperated very generously. The county supervisors lent their road graders and tractors for trenching work. Offices were furnished to the force by the chamber of commerce.

All local slaughterhouses were closed with the exception of those which could be provided with ante-mortem and post-mortem inspections by the State.

As each infection appeared, the Bureau of Biological Survey at once sent out a representative and surrounded the infection with poisoned bait. This helped to prevent the outbreak from being spread by predatory animals.

MOVING STOCK TO FORESTS

The eastern portion of Madera County lies in the Sierra National Forest, on which many herds are pastured during the summer season. At the time the disease appeared in Madera County the herds were almost in readiness for this move. Being accustomed to go to the forest each year, these cattle, when short of feed as they were in 1924, would break fences and proceed by themselves. It was desirable, therefore, to arrange some safe method for moving the stock, and a public meeting of all permittees—those having permit to use the forest range—was called. At this meeting the permittees voiced their cooperation and accepted the plan of action, which was briefly as follows:

A " deadline " was established across the county, far enough from the border of the national forest to include most of the permittees. Then guards who were under the complete jurisdiction of a Federal inspector were appointed to patrol this line constantly and roads back as far as the forest border. Although no roads were closed, the people kept themselves under voluntary quarantine. People wishing to pass through this district on the highways met with no opposition from the guards but were requested not to stop anywhere in it. The plan of action was based on the knowledge that, if stock in the district were already exposed, some animals would show the disease before time to enter the forest, a matter of 20 days hence. Also if it were known that during that time no person left the district and no person stopped within the district, these facts, together with an observed healthy condition of the stock, would make the movement safe.

On May 20 the necessary inspections of the stock began. After receiving two inspections, each by a different inspector, a herd was scheduled to leave its home ranch on a certain hour of a specified day and proceed to the forest border where it received a third inspection. This gave a definite check on each inspector as well as three inspections of the stock. The herds began their movements as scheduled and entered the forest in perfect clockwork order. After all this stock had entered the forest, it was held by riders for further inspections. Two and sometimes three were made, after which the animals were allowed their freedom. No disease appeared. The splendid cooperation of the Forest Service made the successful movement of the herds to the forest possible.

DROUGHT CONDITIONS

The severe drought worked a hardship on those herds of Madera County which were being held under quarantine. It was necessary for some owners to purchase feed; and, because of shortage of water, some quarantined herds had to be moved to other pastures where water could be obtained. In these emergency cases a close study of the local conditions was made so that the movement would involve the least possible risk.

CARCASS DISPOSAL

The chief difficulty in digging trenches to receive the infected stock was due to hardpan. It was necessary in some instances to use explosives to shatter and loosen it before the trench-digging equipment could operate. Steam shovels proved their value, both in speed and economy, in most of the digging operations. When burying large herds, a road grader drawn by a caterpillar tractor proved to be very successful in filling the trenches. Such a scraper makes an extremely neat job of mounding the earth, and this point is greatly appreciated by the owner of the land.

Comparatively little of the infection in Madera County was in the portion containing dairy ranches; however, the regulations adopted in other infected communities were enforced in this county. Managers of dairies were instructed to leave their cans containing milk or cream on the roadside, and creamery trucks, which gathered the products, were not permitted to enter the premises. All establishments handling dairy products were required to disinfect the cans thoroughly before returning them, and inspections were made every day or two to see that the regulations were obeyed.

MOVING HAY, WOOL, HIDES, AND PELTS

When the quarantine was imposed on Madera County, the movement of such farm products as hay, wool, hides, and pelts was permitted only in accordance with Federal and State regulations. Wool from places where infection was found was disinfected with formaldehyde gas in an air-tight room and then permitted to go immediately to some scouring plant.

Madera County was first quarantined on account of foot-and-mouth disease on May 6, 1924. The first modification of quarantine was made June 5, and the final release, with the exception of premises on which infection had existed, was made July 17.

The outbreak of foot-and-mouth disease in San Francisco County was noteworthy for the small number of animals infected, and for the speed in stamping it out. At 9.30 a. m., March 24, a hog in a packing establishment in " Butchertown," San Francisco, was found in one of the company's holding pens with well-marked lesions of the disease.

The plant was immediately quarantined; the pen involved was washed and disinfected; all employees were ordered to disinfect their footwear and not to leave the pens until after changing their clothes. No one was allowed to come near the hog under suspicion until the arrival of inspectors experienced in diagnosing the disease, which was about noon. These men in consultation pronounced the case foot-and-mouth disease. The entire packing plant was surrounded with police; all trucks and cars coming into and leaving the plant were run through a pool of water which contained 3 per cent of cresol solution; all caretakers of animals were well fumigated before leaving the plant for their homes; and the Union Stock Yards were quarantined.

Ten hogs regarded as possibly infected were slaughtered in the pen which contained them, soaked with cresol and " tanked " under Federal supervision. The pen was thoroughly disinfected. Hogs in the plant were slaughtered as quickly as possible under United States inspection, but as most of the hogs were well isolated from the pen containing the infected hog, the exposure was not considered great. All street clothes worn by plant laborers were fumigated every day until the plant was cleaned and disinfected.

On March 26 three more hogs were found in a pen near the first case of infection, all three showing well-marked hoof lesions. These animals and a suspect, in addition, were killed in the pen, thoroughly disinfected and tanked under supervision. The following day five additional hogs in an adjoining pen developed severe lameness and were killed and tanked.

The 12 packing plants that were placed under quarantine in the district were not allowed to receive any more stock for either slaughter or feeding purposes until all animals then in their feed lots and packing pens had been slaughtered and the plant cleaned and disinfected.

Investigation led to the following history of the infection. The shipment of hogs in which the disease was found had been loaded at Merced on March 19. It consisted of 116 hogs purchased in the vicinity of that town. They were brought from ranches to the railroad corral. It was learned later that infected cattle had occupied the corral. The hogs, however, had not been driven over any infected road nor was any infection found at any time on premises from which they had been gathered. The evidence is conclusive that they picked up the infection in the corral in which they were held before being loaded.

When seen by the Federal veterinarian while making his inspections in the holding pens of the packing plant, the first diseased hog was lying down and refused to stand. Examination revealed swelling and tenderness of the coronary bands of three feet; the integument was broken but no vesicles were present. Yet the general behavior of the hog was that of an acute case of foot-and-mouth disease. The lesions of the coronary regions of three feet were typical of the lesions of that disease, immediately following the vesicular stage. No lameness had been observed by either the attendants or bureau inspectors who had observed the hogs at the time of unloading and had inspected them several times after arrival. Thus, there were two factors pointing toward the disease: (1) Abrupt onset of the lameness without other cause, and (2) the knowledge that the hogs originated in an area in which the disease had recently developed.

The usual procedure would have been to quarantine the premises and await developments, warranting an unqualified diagnosis. But the conditions in this case were extraordinary. These animals were in packers' pens surrounded by hundreds of other animals and in the immediate vicinity were the pens of 11 other packers containing other hundreds of susceptible animals. Within a radius of a mile were thousands of animals in feed lots and large numbers of animals were arriving daily by train and truck. It required no stretch of imagination to realize that delay might mean a disastrous spread of the disease. These conditions demanded the immediate slaughter of the affected and exposed animals and other action taken as already described.

The stockyards were cleaned and disinfected and livestock shipments resumed April 2, 1924. The outbreak may be considered as lasting but a day in the dangerous stage, though disinfection was not completed until a week later. The work in this locality was conducted without undue excitement and with little inconvenience to the public.

THE LOS ANGELES OUTBREAK

The first discovery of foot-and-mouth disease in southern California was in Los Angeles County. San Bernardino was the second, and Orange the third of the southern counties to be affected. On March 24, 1924, the disease was detected on the premises of three packing companies. On discovery of the infection, the Los Angeles Union Stock Yards Co. refused to accept more livestock and directed commission firms operating in the yards to sell for slaughter all susceptible animals that remained in the yards. When the yards were cleared of livestock they were thoroughly cleaned for disinfection. Railroad companies were notified to stop shipments of livestock billed to Los Angeles that had left their points of origin and to locate for cleaning and disinfecting all livestock cars that had been used in Los Angeles County in transporting livestock. All packers in Los Angeles and the suburb, Vernon, were urged to slaughter for food as soon as possible all susceptible animals that were being held on feed on their premises.

Slaughterhouses in Los Angeles County outside of Los Angeles and Vernon were ordered closed and auction sales of livestock were prohibited. Owners of livestock were urged to avoid moving animals until the extent of the disease had been determined. A Government order quarantining Los Angeles County became effective March 25.

The conditions under which the disease broke out merit a brief description. Thirteen independent packing plants are on East Vernon

Avenue, in the town of Vernon, adjacent to the city of Los Angeles. This packing-house row is not more than a mile long and at a number of places the stock pens of various concerns adjoin one another. The Los Angeles Union Stock Yards are about one-half mile to the east of the end of the row mentioned. Animals purchased at the yards for slaughter are driven or trucked over East Vernon Avenue. Farmers and livestock speculators who operate on a small scale frequently haul by truck to these slaughtering establishments loads of calves, dry cows, sheep, or hogs and offer them for direct sale to the packers. A seller frequently proceeds along the entire length of the street, seeking a satisfactory bid. It is also a common practice for the large packing concerns to send buyers into the country and purchase livestock in lots of from 1 to 30 carloads to be delivered at a specified time. Some of these animals are slaughtered at once, others being kept on feed in the pens of the packing companies until they are in good flesh or until there is a demand for that particular kind of meat.

In addition to the 13 packing plants mentioned, 3 other plants are within the city limits of Los Angeles. Two of these operate under Federal inspection and the third under city inspection. A short distance north of the stockyards a large herd of dairy cattle was kept. The owners speculated in dairy stock and many persons visited the farm almost daily to buy dairy cattle, to return animals found unsatisfactory, to breed cows, and to buy calves for veal. Separated only by a railroad right of way from this dairy farm is a feeding plant covering approximately 32 acres and operated by a large milling company. Various owners consign cattle to these feed yards to be fed cottonseed hulls and cottonseed meal. From 60 to 120 days is the customary time of feeding. There were approximately 10,000 head of livestock either on feed or awaiting slaughter within the same area of the Vernon district when foot-and-mouth disease was discovered there. Under these conditions the eradication compaign was begun in southern California. It will be readily understood that there had been much movement of livestock, persons, rodents, pigeons, meat, hides, and like products before the eradication forces were organized. Therefore it is not surprising that the disease gained entrance to practically all herds in the locality as well as in the packing-house and stockyards district.

Infected animals were slaughtered and buried in the customary manner. Inspectors were assigned to sort out exposed animals and those not showing lesions. These were loaded in railroad cars lined with tar paper and shipped to the various packing plants for slaughter under rigid inspection.

When all infected and exposed herds in the Vernon district had been disposed of, the packing houses suspended operations in order that their premises might be cleaned and disinfected. On April 20— less than a month from the time of original infection—the Union Stock Yards Co., and the packing plants that had been cleaned and disinfected were permitted to resume operations with the understanding that no livestock was to remain alive longer than 48 hours after its arrival. To prevent the arrival of more livestock than could be absorbed by the packers, a control committee was organized. This committee consisted of one livestock producer, one representative of the packers, one representative of the railroads, the market supervisor employed by the packers and stockyards administration, and a veterinarian representing the California Department of Agriculture. The committee estimated the number and classes of livestock that could be slaughtered within 48 hours after its arrival and issued permits to railroads and truck companies to deliver the proper quantity of livestock for each day's demands. The livestock received was from both quarantined and free areas.

State and bureau inspectors were assigned at the Union Stock Yards and at the packing plants to inspect stock on its arrival, to supervise the cleaning and disinfection of trucks and cars that were used in transporting livestock, and to enforce the 48-hour killing requirement. Livestock arriving during the night was held in cars until daylight in order that it might be inspected as soon as it was unloaded. Railroad companies and trucking companies were required to furnish equipment with tight floors and sides for transporting livestock from quarantined areas to market. The loading of livestock at the point of origin in a quarantined area was supervised by a State or bureau inspector; no animals were loaded for market until all stock on the original premises had been inspected immediately before the loading commenced. The stockyards company installed extra trackage and other facilities for washing and disinfecting all cars and trucks that were used in transporting livestock to market and delivering livestock from the yards to the packing plants.

Under this plan an outlet to market was furnished for livestock within quarantined areas and slaughtering establishments were allowed to conduct their business, except for the short period when they were closed for cleaning and disinfection. No spread of infection resulted from this handling of livestock and no infected animals were observed in the yards or at the packing plants while this system was in force.

On April 3 infection was discovered among garbage-fed hogs on a ranch in the Lankershim district, approximately 20 miles from the Vernon district where foot-and-mouth disease was first discovered in Los Angeles County. It is believed that infected garbage was responsible for the disease on this ranch. Evidently the infection was of several days' standing when it was discovered, as the hoofs of several of the affected hogs were sloughing. In various ways the disease gained access to numerous herds of cattle in the vicinity, also to one small herd of hogs.

On April 3, the same day that infection was found in the Lankershim district, the disease appeared in two herds of cattle in a locality known as the Inglewood district. This outbreak was rather limited, involving only five premises.

Another district known as Lamanda Park became infected April 7, when a large dairy herd in it "broke" with the disease. A day later the infection appeared on another farm. From that time up to May 12 numerous other herds of cattle and also several lots of goats contracted the malady. One of the first farms in this district to be involved had received cattle from the Union Stock Yards a few days before they were quarantined. This was the probable source of infection.

The spread of infection in the Lamanda Park district was aided by the closeness of the premises to one another. In some cases they adjoined, whereas in others they were separated only by a narrow street or alley. The dairymen were inclined to visit one another; pigeons and rodents moved about freely; and all the feed used for the dairy cattle was shipped in and delivered to the various dairies. Under those conditions it was difficult to trace the means of infection in every case.

Another portion of Los Angeles County to be extensively involved in the outbreak was the Downey-Hynes district. Infection of very virulent nature was detected there on April 14, but apparently several other herds were exposed before the case was discovered, for they broke with the disease a short time later. The infection continued to spread and new herds became involved every few days until July 29. The Los Angeles County farm was among the premises affected.

On April 22 foot-and-mouth disease was discovered among the hogs that ate Long Beach city garbage on the premises of the Long Beach garbage farm. Difficulty was experienced in getting these hogs buried for the reason that the steam shovel used in digging the trench was not in good repair and also that water pipes were broken during the digging operation.

DIFFICULTIES OF APPRAISAL

The appraisal of herds in Los Angeles County involved unusual difficulties, even though nearly all the appraisals were made by the same men for the purpose of obtaining the greatest uniformity. Many of the dairy cattle had been sold on time payments at very high prices with but little money paid on them. With several sellers holding mortgages on the cattle the appraisers experienced considerable difficulty in arriving at satisfactory values. In a number of cases it was especially difficult to get all the necessary signatures on claim papers and affidavits in order that the legal claims of all interested parties might be protected. In several instances men in charge of infected herds represented to the appraisers that they held full title to the cattle when later it developed that the cattle were heavily mortgaged.

TRENCH DIGGING

Except where large herds were to be buried, steam shovels proved to be an expensive and unsatisfactory means of excavating. The operators expected pay for the time used in moving the machine to and from the premises where the work was to be done. Occasionally one would break or get stuck in mud or sand en route. When water was encountered within a few feet of the surface, a steam shovel was almost useless. The use of teams, scrapers, and hand labor was generally satisfactory when a reliable man was given the contract for digging and refilling the trench. Usually laborers and teams were kept on the premises from the time the excavating was begun until the burial of the animals was completed, meals being brought to the laborers.

OTHER DIFFICULTIES ENCOUNTERED

In Los Angeles County numerous persons of foreign birth were engaged in various branches of the dairy business. Many of them were not inclined to look on foot-and-mouth disease as a serious proposition and it was difficult to convince them that strict compliance with the State and Federal regulations was essential if the disease was to be eradicated. Inspectors were directed to inform livestock owners concerning the various ways in which infection spreads and to urge those in charge of susceptible animals to use every available means of preventing infection from reaching their herds. To aid in obtaining this result the secretary of the Southern California Milk Producers' Association agreed to refuse to handle the milk of any member who willfully violated regulations. It was necessary to use this leverage in three instances in Los Angeles County. In various parts of the county arrests were made for violations, and fines of from $5 to $50 were imposed.

Experience in digging graves where the water was near the surface is of interest in view of possible future problems of this kind. In the *Downey-Hynes* district an attempt was made to dig a trench with a steam shovel, but at a depth of about 3 feet water was encountered. The water was bailed out and the job completed with hand shovels. When the trench was completed most of the water was removed and the cattle brought to the side of the trench where they were slaughtered and dragged into the trench. When other small herds in the vicinity became infected, individual graves were dug for the stock so that water could be removed from the trenches as fast as they were dug.

HANDLING DAIRY PRODUCTS

To prevent the possible spread of infection through milk, State dairy inspectors were assigned to supervise Pasteurization of milk at the creameries and pay particular attention to the sterilization of cans and bottles. At several creameries it was observed that only the insides of the cans were sterilized by inverting the empty can over a jet of live steam for perhaps a fourth of a minute. This method was considered unsatisfactory and creameries were required to provide facilities that would insure a thorough sterilization of the entire can and can cover, inside and outside.

Drivers of milk trucks were required to clean and disinfect their trucks on delivering their loads of milk at the creameries and to cover the floors of the trucks with chloride of lime. Then the truck driver was required to start from the creamery dressed in clean clothing, including clean cotton gloves, and to deliver all the empty cans at the roadside before any full milk cans were loaded. The truck drivers were not allowed to deliver hay or feed on the trucks used in handling milk. This precaution prevented the possibility of empty cans becoming contaminated by contact with cans from an infected farm not yet discovered. Delivery of cans and collection of milk at the roadside were strictly enforced.

ORIGIN OF THE INFECTION

The outbreak of foot-and-mouth disease in Los Angeles County, investigation showed, was due to the shipment of two carloads of cattle from Merced prior to the time that the disease was detected there. These cattle were driven about 6 miles to the railroad corrals and in being driven that distance they traveled a little more than half a mile over the same road that had been used by infected cattle the previous day in traveling between two ranches. These two carloads of cattle were the ones that carried the infection to Los Angeles. The manner in which the disease was picked up and carried shows clearly the many possibilities of spreading the disease.

TESTING AND RESTOCKING PREMISES

Test animals were placed on very few premises in southern California earlier than 60 days after cleaning and disinfection had been completed. Before test animals were placed on premises a veterinary inspector examined the buildings and surroundings, and if repairs were necessary, instructed the owner to make repairs in buildings, fences, and gates so that the test animals could not escape. When the premises were in satisfactory condition the inspector issued a certificate to that effect so there need be no delay in starting the test as soon as quarantine conditions permitted.

DISPOSAL OF MANURE

Since barnyard manure in southern California is much in demand as fertilizer for orange groves, vineyards, and lawns it was evident that the manure would be widely distributed when it was released from previously infected premises. Therefore, unless the fertilizer could be removed from those premises and disposed of without danger of spreading infection, it remained on the premises until the test animals had had access to it 30 days or more. Both pigs and cattle were used as test animals on premises that were equipped to hold pigs. No calves under 6 months old were recognized as test animals. These animals were inspected daily for the first two weeks and then at gradually increasing intervals up to twice a week until 90 days had elapsed. After a successful 30-day test period owners were permitted to increase the number of animals on the premises gradually until the full capacity was attained or the premises released from quarantine. Owners were notified that previously infected premises and animals placed on them would be kept under quarantine for at least 90 days. Infected premises on which no test animals were placed after cleaning and disinfection were not released until January 1, 1925.

METHOD OF TESTING SAFETY OF HAY

In the dairy districts of Los Angeles and Orange Counties little hay is produced; therefore it is necessary for dairymen to ship in most of the hay and feed for cattle. These products were delivered to the dairies at the roadside to avoid having the trucks and drivers enter the premises. On some infected premises hayfields were adjacent to the cattle corrals. If infected animals had been kept out of the hayfields, permission was granted owners to harvest the hay and stack it in the field, leaving a strip approximately 100 feet around the infected corrals and barns to be cut and kept separate from the rest of the hay and to be used for feeding the test animals when they were placed on the premises. Permits were not issued to move hay stored in barns on infected premises or the hay harvested outside the 100-foot strip on infected premises until a successful 30-day test period had elapsed.

Altogether 280 herds were infected in Los Angeles County. In Orange County the outbreak was much less extensive, being limited to 23 herds. These herds were found to be infected between May 2 and May 26, the last one being slaughtered and buried May 28.

OUTBREAK IN SAN BERNARDINO COUNTY

In San Bernardino County the disease was discovered on April 21 in the pens of a company that probably feeds more hogs on garbage than any other firm in this country. At that time this company had over 40,000 hogs on or near the premises where the infected animals were being fed. As soon as the disease was diagnosed the 760 animals in the first infected unit—containing 10 pens of approximately 75 animals each—were immediately killed and buried and the usual precautions taken to prevent the spread of the infection to other units. However, the infection did reach a second unit, containing 748 hogs, having been carried by a laborer who was assisting in inoculating test animals, in a small animal hospital maintained on the premises, with material obtained from pigs in the first unit before a definite diagnosis had been reached. On being requested to get another pig for inoculation purposes, he unfortunately went directly from the hospital to a pen in the second unit to obtain a pig, and evidently carried the virus on his shoes, as the disease appeared in this second unit a few days later. However, the infection was controlled by April 28 and further spread of the disease to the other units was prevented. The miraculous escape of these remaining hogs shows the desirability of making every reasonable effort to save healthy animals, especially when large numbers are involved and conditions and facilities appear to make the effort feasible.

OUTBREAK IN TUOLUMNE COUNTY

In Tuolumne County the first report of foot-and-mouth disease was received April 6, 1924. Three inspectors proceeded to the premises, near Sonora, early the next day. Drooling and lameness were observed in several cows and young calves but other symptoms of foot-and-mouth disease were absent. Since the cattle were fairly well isolated in a 10-acre lot it was decided to hold them in this small inclosure for future observation. Meanwhile the inspection force examined all cattle on ranges bordering the one on which the affected cattle had grazed but found no other animals affected.

Since the cattle held for observation were the first in the county to show symptoms resembling foot-and-mouth disease, it was decided to conduct tests to determine the nature of the ailment. Tests made with six young, thrifty pigs failed to show signs of foot-and-mouth disease. The pigs remained normal and increased in weight until killed, May 17.

Meanwhile, during the progress of the test, cattle on another range showed symptoms of a disease suspected to be foot-and-mouth disease. A visit to the locality known as the Duckwell range confirmed the suspicion. The inspection of the suspected cattle occurred at 6 a. m., May 7, and 25 cattle showed symptoms of foot-and-mouth disease. The range was immediately quarantined. This range, already mentioned in connection with the deer situation, is in the Stanislaus National Forest and about 20 miles east of Sonora, Calif. The infection was brought to this range by cattle which were driven from their home ranch, in the southern part of the county.

The evidence shows that the disease was brought into Tuolumne County from Stanislaus County, on the south. A ranch employee who assisted in branding cattle preparatory to taking them to the range in the national forest had come shortly before from a ranch in Stanislaus County, where the disease had existed.

On May 9 another herd showed signs of the disease and during the week beginning May 11, 11 additional herds became infected. They were disposed of the same week. Still another herd showed symptoms on May 20 and was slaughtered and buried that day.

Following several weeks of apparent suppression, another outbreak occurred July 2, the infection having evidently been carried over by one or more estrays. Many herds were exposed by the infected herd and were quarantined along the route of travel, the inspectors using every precaution in spacing diseased and exposed herds from healthy herds.

TRENCH PREPARATION

Since there were no contractors in Tuolumne County, the task of preparing trenches to receive the diseased stock was an added problem for the inspection force. It was necessary to borrow implements and scour the country for horses and laborers, though splendid cooperation was received from local business firms which had teams and digging equipment. An added difficulty was the rough, rocky, and mountainous nature of the country, which made trench construction unusually difficult.

Burial pits, inspected by the county health officer, were bulkheaded and ditched to meet his approval and to prevent contamination of the great storage reservoirs from which the cities of the valley derive their water supply. The pits also were inspected frequently to insure their maintenance in good condition.

The range in Tuolumne County where infection was encountered was not only rough and difficult of access, even on horseback, but was heavily wooded and presented the superlative of difficulties both as to inspection of livestock and gathering them in their entirety when necessary. There were no fences worthy of the name, and straying and mingling of herds on different ranges were common. The disposition of cattle on the Duckwell range of the Stanislaus National Forest, as well as all subsequent burying in that forest, was attended with greater difficulty, by far, than any other such operation in the California campaign. The altitude is about 6,000 feet, and to reach this range it was necessary to travel about 10 miles of narrow, mountain-side roadway. To obtain trenching machinery, teams, and large numbers of laborers was out of the question. Only one solution presented itself with any degree of practicability and that consisted in seeking out deep, natural gulleys, abandoned cuts of logging railways, and deserted prospect pits, where the drainage could be diverted, placing the animals in them and covering the carcasses, after slaughter, by blasting in the walls. Herds were large, numbering usually from 100 to 500 head.   All the trenches were safeguarded against flood damage by putting in diverting dams and running ditches around them.   The necessity of building corrals to receive and hold the cattle pending their slaughter added still further to the work of eradication.

The speed with which foot-and-mouth disease spread in Tuolumne County following its diagnosis on May 9 is seen by the fact that the disease was discovered on 14 ranges in 14 days from the first infection and extending over a distance of nearly 50 miles.   But so rapidly did the men work that they had made not only a complete inspection of all the livestock for a distance of more than 60 miles but had destroyed and buried the 14 infected herds, some of them in the most difficult mountainous country imaginable, within the short period of two weeks.

Early in the outbreak it was discovered that, because of the very rough, timbered, and brushy, mountainous country from which the cattle would have to be gathered, there would be a large number of stray animals left.   In order to meet this condition, which from an eradication standpoint was a very serious one, a number of picked veterinarians, each with an assistant who knew the country, were equipped with high-powered rifles and instructed to rid the range of these strays.   This work was not completed until early in the fall. Just how thoroughly the hills were "combed" by these men is told in the words "not one stray made its escape from the mountains to the foothills."

A still further problem that confronted the work was a serious drought.   Because of the lack of snow and rain during the winter and spring, there was a scarcity of water and feed in all pastures in the foothills and valleys.   This necessitated the removal of the cattle to the mountain ranges a month earlier than under normal conditions, as practically all streams were dry and green feed gone by the 1st of June.

On May 1 detailed plans were announced, rules of procedure adopted, and a number of veterinarians assigned to make inspections of animals for movement to the summer ranges in the various national forests.   It was agreed that no livestock from counties quarantined for foot-and-mouth disease would be permitted to enter the forests.

In accordance with plans involving the most painstaking precautions to prevent the spread of infection, healthy herds were permitted to move along specified routes to mountain pastures.   Inspectors examined the cattle early each morning, in the corrals, and continued the inspection throughout the day.   Herds that were in close proximity to infected areas were moved within the county and held for safe periods before continuing the trip to the mountains, being inspected at frequent intervals.   Finally, before the cattle were permitted to be turned loose on the range, they were given a final inspection during a period of from 7 to 10 days.   The inspectors instructed the cattlemen that the entire herd that left a point of origin must be accounted for each night; and, in the event that any animals became too tired or for some other reason could not travel, they were to be put into an inclosure to prevent their straying into infected territory.

On May 2, 1924, a condition resembling foot-and-mouth disease was discovered among cattle in Tulare County, Calif. It occurred on a dairy ranch 7 miles west and 3 miles north of Porterville of that county and was reported by a practicing veterinarian. Examination by bureau veterinarians led to no positive diagnosis, there being a marked resemblance to necrotic stomatitis. Tests were conducted with pigs and a calf, resulting, however, on May 7, in a positive diagnosis of foot-and-mouth disease. The stock on the premises consisted of 130 cattle and 72 hogs. During the period May 2 to May 16 the disease appeared on five other premises in the neighborhood. In each case all the susceptible animals were slaughtered and buried, usually within a day or two of the time of discovery. The last of these herds was buried May 18.

No further " breaks " of foot-and-mouth disease occurred in Tulare County until June 16, when it appeared among 76 cattle and 67 hogs on a ranch; these animals were slaughtered and buried June 19.

There is no definite evidence to show how the infection was brought into Tulare County. But the probable source was the presence of calf buyers from Los Angeles in the neighborhood of the first infected ranch a week before the disease appeared. Infection was carried to two other herds by their owners, who admitted having assisted in treating sick animals in the first herd affected before a veterinarian was called. Further spread of foot-and-mouth disease in the locality was traced principally to the mingling of cattle.

The plan of eradication included dividing the territory into sections of convenient size for inspections and house-to-house inspection for a distance of 5 miles out from the infection. At the time the outbreak occurred the county had been operating for a considerable time under a quarantine imposed by the county board of supervisors. Supplying guards was under the direct supervision of the county horticultural commissioner. As soon as the disease was discovered on a farm a guard was immediately available. There was a permanent camp at the edge of the infected area, where all guards were housed and fed. A telephone line connected the camp with the headquarters office in Porterville, so that there was direct touch with the infected area day and night.

The construction of trenches was taken over by the board of supervisors at practically cost price. All slaughterhouses within the quarantined area were closed and no slaughtering was conducted until such time as the State was able to furnish inspectors working under the California meat-inspection law.

The principal difficulties encountered were those due to the severe drought. Feed conditions were deplorable, especially in the section adjacent to the national forest. However, the quarantine was removed on May 26 from the portion of Tulare County bordering on the national forest; this served in a measure to relieve the conditions and to permit the movement of stock to the national forest.

The creameries in Tulare County cooperated with the eradication forces by Pasteurizing at the receiving point all milk and cream from the quarantined area. Movement of hay, wool, and like products was permitted only under special permit.

11858°—26——4

OUTBREAK IN FRESNO COUNTY

In Fresno County foot-and-mouth disease was first discovered May 12, 1924, in a pasture herd on a ranch 6 miles northeast of Clovis. Fresno was the last county in the State in which the disease made its appearance and was the last county to be quarantined. The owner, who was a woman, noticed on the date mentioned that her stock appeared to be sick and notified the county livestock inspector by telephone. He visited the ranch immediately and after quarantining the premises returned to Fresno and reported to the Sacramento office that the animals showed symptoms indicating foot-and-mouth disease. L. Enos *D*ay, an expert diagnostician, arrived at the ranch the following day, confirmed the diagnosis, and so informed official headquarters at Sacramento.

Two Federal inspectors had been assigned to Fresno County, before the "break" occurred, for the purpose of inspecting cattle and sheep entering the national forests for summer pasturage. Being informed of the break they visited the ranch to investigate recent movements of cattle in the vicinity. They learned that cattle had been moved recently from the infected ranch to a foothill ranch, 2 miles to the northeast, operated by the same owner. That herd also was found to be infected. These veterinary inspectors also learned that a heifer had been moved from the first ranch to a herd in a dairy district about 10 miles south. An inspection of that herd was made but no evidence of the disease was found. However, the heifer was killed and buried as a precautionary measure.

Referring again to the first herd found to be infected, the disease spread to the hogs on the ranch. The severe lameness of infected hogs and numerous well marked, typical lesions in various stages on the membranes of the mouths of cattle indicated that the infection was of the most virulent type.

The disease spread rapidly to other ranches in instances in which direct exposure could be traced. However, its spread was confined to ranches adjoining those on which the original infection was found. This is rather remarkable, for three of the herds were of the most dangerous kind, from a disease-eradication standpoint. They were public-pasturage herds where traders, dealers, and various owners had been accustomed to meet to transact cattle deals. What little spread of infection occurred was traced to several causes, such as mingling of cattle because of poor fences, feeding calves milk from cows later found to be infected, and movement of herds to pastures containing stock that later developed the disease. The presence of coyotes in the region may account for some spread of infection. Other suspected carriers were buzzards, squirrels, and high winds, but no conclusive facts support these suspicions.

ORGANIZATION OF FORCE

The chief branches of the force of eradication included an inspection crew, killing crew, and disinfection crew. The infected area was divided into six districts of convenient size and a veterinary inspector assigned to each with instructions to make daily, semiweekly, or weekly inspections, depending on the extent of exposure, of all susceptible animals in those territories. Under this arrangement all susceptible animals were inspected at least once a week in each district.

The method greatly facilitated the inspection of animals for immediate slaughter, as an owner needed only to apply to the district inspector for an examination, obtain a permit for movement for immediate slaughter, and deliver the animals to point of slaughter or shipment. The plan was effective later, also, when stock was allowed to move to the national forests for summer pasture. Under this plan cattle were moved with assurance as to their healthy condition.

APPRAISALS

Appraisals of infected herds were made by three appraisers, representing the Federal Government, State, and the owner, respectively. Most of the infected cattle in this county were range cattle and most of the herds destroyed were pasture herds belonging to various owners. It was necessary to have the State brand inspector present at appraisals to establish ownership of the animals. Sometimes an owner or other person best qualified represented the various owners during the appraising; it was too dangerous to permit numerous owners on infected premises, if effective control of the disease was to be had. In some instances owners were absent from the county or State and could not be reached quickly. Most of the animals slaughtered were mortgaged and some delay was experienced in submitting all necessary papers for payment. The appraisals were well conducted and no slaughtering was delayed by interference from any owner.

Guards used in the county were hired and supervised by the county livestock inspector. An efficient organization was in operation when the Federal and State forces arrived and it was continued throughout the emergency.

DIGGING EQUIPMENT

Three outfits for digging were ordered into service by the county livestock inspector before the arrival of the Federal and State eradication forces. These outfits included road equipment, teams, plows, scoops, scrapers, steam shovels, and operators. Most of the herds were buried in trenches in the customary manner; but some animals were buried in an abandoned copper-mine shaft. (Fig. 7.)

ROAD DIPS

Several disinfecting dips were in operation on roads in Fresno County before the first infection was discovered. County officials believed that this precaution might prevent infection from being brought in from other counties. This plan was gradually abandoned. Spray pumps with which to disinfect contacting surfaces of automobiles, other vehicles, horses' and mules' feet were being used before Federal authorities arrived but were later abandoned except when automobiles and teams came from infected premises.

COUNTY QUARANTINE

County officials placed many premises under provisional quarantine long before the first herd was known to be infected. This was done in cases of herds regarded as suspicious and to prevent persons from entering such premises. It proved to be very effective.

LOCAL SLAUGHTERING PLACES

There was but one slaughterhouse in the quarantined area and it was closed during the entire quarantine period. Several packing houses and abattoirs were in operation in the free areas of Fresno County. All but one were operated under inspection furnished or supervised by State officials.

FOREST SERVICE

The supervisors of the Sierra and Sequoia National Forests rendered much valuable assistance. Rangers from their forces fur-

FIG. 7.—Burying a carcass in an abandoned mine shaft. This method of disposing of animals affected with foot-and-mouth disease was used in a mining district where the soil was unusually rocky

nished transportation and acted as guides for inspectors when examining herds prior to movement into the forests. These rangers knew the ranches and ranchers in the locality and were of great help in locating and arranging for the inspection of herds.

FREE AREA ABOUT INFECTED AREA

An area free of susceptible animals was established between the infected area and the national forests. Natural free areas existed to the south and west, as these were vineyard sections. The San Joaquin River served as a barrier on the north. The free area on the east was established by ranch owners who moved their livestock east or west to cause an area from north to south from 1 to 2 miles in width. This free area was maintained until the danger of spread of the disease toward the forests had passed. In fact it was greatly enlarged later, when those herds were moved to the forests for summer pasture.

The outbreak occurred in and was confined to the north-central part of the county. The county is nearly flat through the central portion known as the San Joaquin Valley, but breaks abruptly into the foothills, gradually extending to high mountain ranges at the western and eastern ends of the county. Vineyards and fig orchards cover most of the valley area but the foothills and mountains are adapted only for cattle and sheep ranges.

Most of the livestock were on the foothills ranges. Many of the vineyard ranches kept no livestock at all: some kept only a cow or a

Fig. 8.—Inspection of range cattle. The inspector (right) is pointing out a suspected animal for the riders to rope for a closer examination

few pigs. The greatest danger was the spread of the disease through the foothill country into the national forests, where thousands of head of cattle and sheep were on pasture; and the general movement of livestock was in that direction during the spring of the year.

The herds in the Fresno district were large, ranging from 100 to 1,000 or more cattle. Not many bands of sheep were kept in the quarantined area. Ranges were large, consisting usually of from 1,000 to 15,000 acres. Fences were constructed mostly of only three strands of barbed wire, which often became loosened from the posts and were ineffective for confining livestock. Every infected herd had strays that had wandered from some other ranch. So far as disease eradication was concerned, the foothill ranches, fenced as described, were practically open range. Consequently it was necessary to have riders round up all the animals in infected herds, including strays that mingled with the herd, in order to be certain that none escaped slaughter.

MOVEMENT OF LIVESTOCK AND PRODUCTS

Every effort was made to have fat animals moved under permit for immediate slaughter when it could be done safely. Such animals were moved locally to Fresno slaughterhouses or to points of shipment for Los Angeles or San Francisco markets. The movement of hay, straw, wool, and similar products was done under written permits issued by State inspectors.

MOVEMENT OF LIVESTOCK INTO NATIONAL FORESTS

Cattle and sheep were permitted to enter the national forest ranges only after receiving three rigid inspections during a period of 10 days from the first inspection to the last. (Fig. 8.) All suspected animals that could not be restrained otherwise were roped and tied for rigid inspection before a herd was passed on any of the inspec-

Fig. 9.—Making a veterinary inspection, on the range, of an animal suspected of being infected with foot-and-mouth disease. Experience in riding, roping, and restraining unruly stock is a necessary qualification for employees engaged in eradication work

tions. (Fig. 9.) A total of 10,140 cattle were inspected before entering the forest during the assignment of the Federal veterinary forces in that county. Most of the sheep in the county were in the free area in the western part of the San Joaquin Valley. Altogether 12,665 sheep were inspected, loaded, and shipped in sealed cars through the quarantined area into the free area in the national forest, where they were again inspected as unloaded.

METHODS OF INSPECTION

Two systems of inspecting range herds were used in the examination of exposed cattle or those suspected of being diseased. Each has its good points. One is to have riders—who may be furnished by the owner—round up all animals, hold them until the inspector arrives, then cut them back along a fence or other barrier one at a time, pa t the inspector, so that he can count and observe each one. (Fig. 10s)

The good features of this method are as follows: One inspector can confine all his efforts to inspecting cattle instead of spending

90 per cent of his time hunting cattle. He can also count the animals in each herd. Suspicious animals can be roped, tied, and thoroughly examined at once. About three times as many animals can be inspected in a day by this method as by riding among the stock scattered over the range. But a bad feature of the system described is that cattle drool naturally after being driven during hot weather, though it can be overcome by allowing them to rest from half an hour to an hour before inspection is made. Animals with sensitive or sore feet may show no signs of lameness after being driven a short distance, but this lameness will return if the animals are rested for 30 minutes or more.

The good features of the system in which the inspector rides among a range herd are that the inspector can ride up to animals lying down, cause them to get up and move about, and observe lameness if it is present. Cattle are always cool when inspected

Fig. 10.—Inspecting a band of sheep for foot-and-mouth disease. Herders drove the sheep slowly between automobile and fence while the inspector watched for lameness, drooling, and other visible signs of the disease

and seldom drool from being overheated. The faults of this system are that every animal will not be observed and an accurate count can not be made. It takes an inspector several days to inspect 1,000 cattle on a 15,000-acre ranch by this method. Sick animals, which are the very ones that the inspector should observe, may be hiding behind a cliff or in the brush and never be seen. The former method is usually preferable since every animal can be observed, it assures immediate diagnosis, and the inspector is more certain when he leaves the herd that it has, or does not have, foot-and-mouth disease. In this connection it may be added that such inspection can be made advantageously from a seat in an automobile. Range livestock are less afraid of a standing automobile and its occupants than they are of men on horseback.

It is evident that care must be exercised in the control and handling of infected range herds. Sufficient riders should be obtained as soon as a herd is known to be infected to make sure that all animals of the herd are gathered and that the herd is under complete control until driven to the trench and slaughtered. It is best not to drive range herds to places for slaughter too late in the day. If darkness overtakes such a herd en route, calves may drop behind unnoticed or the cattle may bolt and some of the animals get away entirely in the darkness and mix with healthy herds.

The graves where infected cattle are buried should be watched closely for at least a month. This is especially important in dry weather, when there is no rain to pack the dirt over the graves. Putrefaction and fermentation of abdominal contents cause an expansion and, when the covering is loose dirt, sometimes a so-called " blowing " of the grave. The procedure in such cases is to cover the openings with chloride of lime and then with earth, afterwards harrowing the surface several times to fill up all cracks and crevices caused by the expansion. Coyotes visiting such graves should be killed off by shooting or poison; 37 dead coyotes were accounted for by these methods in one locality in Fresno County.

HANDLING REPORTS, CLAIMS, AND PAY ROLLS

In suppressing an outbreak of foot-and-mouth disease the actual field activities, such as inspection, slaughter, and burial of infected animals, naturally are well known by the public. But the efficient direction of field forces and proper disposal of indemnity claims and other expenses necessarily depend on accurate, well-kept records. Records are essential also as a basis for answering the many inquiries that constantly arise while eradication work is in progress. The prompt settlement of indemnity claims and other bills depends moreover on obtaining the proper signatures to the different forms and to attention to numerous but necessary details.

The matter of getting the appraisals and indemnity claims in proper form for settlement is specially important. Most owners are eager for their money and, after they have received indemnity checks for animals destroyed, the spirit of cooperation by owners of newly infected herds is a help in getting the new herds quickly disposed off and the premises disinfected.

In preparing indemnity papers, knowledge of the true owners of the stock and whether there are any mortgages or other liens outstanding against the herd is essential. If a mortgage exists, the voucher is stated jointly and signed by the owner of the herd and by the mortgagee; of course the check is made out jointly and mailed to the address given on the voucher.

As a matter of general information relative to mortgages against herds destroyed, the following may be of assistance: Claims covering mortgaged cattle should be stated jointly in favor of the owner, as mortgagor, and of the mortgagee, signed by both, accompanied by a certified copy of mortgage with a statement that the destroyed cattle were the ones covered by the mortgage, that the mortgage has not been paid and that there are no other mortgagees or claimants. A statement, showing where the check should be mailed, should also accompany the claim. In case a mortgage or other paper has been recorded, certified copies of the mortgage must be attached to the voucher regardless of any assignment which has been made.

BILLS FOR FEED AND PASTURE

The question of feed and pasture bills frequently came up for settlement when owners, whose herds were destroyed, owed for feed or pasture consumed by the animals. It was the custom, whenever possible, to have these claims settled by the persons concerned and in most instances this method proved to be satisfactory.

In California it is provided that persons pasturing animals have a lien on the animals for the compensation due for pasturage. This lien, however, is dependent on such persons retaining possession of the animals. If they surrender possession without asserting their lien, then the lien is discharged. If persons having a valid lien on the animals do not relinquish that lien when they surrender possession to the Government for slaughter, the voucher for the indemnity claim is made out jointly and is supported by a certified statement showing the validity of the claim.

HANDLING OF PAY ROLLS AND ACCOUNTS

At the inception of the campaign to eradicate foot-and-mouth disease in California, it became imperative to devise some means to expedite the issuance of pay checks to men hired for a temporary period. This class of labor was used chiefly in connection with the slaughter and burial of livestock and the cleaning and disinfecting of premises. Accordingly arrangements were made between officials of the bureau and the Forest Service whereby A. W. Smith, fiscal agent of the Forest Service, stationed in San Francisco, was authorized to issue checks against funds placed to his credit in the United States Treasury at Washington.

Under this arrangement the men generally received their checks on Tuesday for services rendered during the week ended the previous Thursday evening. When the delay caused by sending pay rolls across the continent to Washington, D. C., for settlement, is realized, the benefits of the foregoing plan for paying temporary laborers are evident. With few exceptions the men employed as laborers had been out of work for some time and were in urgent need of funds. Others were of the itinerant class, working only a few days here and there in order to live and to pay transportation from one place to another. These men were accustomed to receive their pay immediately on quitting the job or on being discharged on completion of the work.

Difficulty was experienced at times in recruiting laborers enough to accomplish the work with dispatch; and any further delay in paying the men would have added to the delay in burying the animals and cleaning and disinfecting the premises promptly.

An outstanding feature in connection with the outbreak in Kern County is the fact that the disease occurred on the headquarters ranch of the Kern County Land Co., one of the largest cattle, sheep, and swine outfits in the West. More than 50 employees were going to and from headquarters daily and they visited all parts of the county attending to cattle, sheep, and irrigation work, without a single extension of the infection. This was one of the few instances in which good fortune appeared to be on the official side. In its zeal to cooperate fully with the State and Federal Governments, the company requested the immediate slaughter of the herd and waived indemnity therefor. All expenses of trenching, cleaning, disinfection, and other items were also borne by the company.

EFFECTS OF OUTBREAK ON INDUSTRY AND COMMERCE

It is well for the reader to bear in mind that an outbreak of an infectious disease causes certain disturbances of industry and commerce in addition to the direct effect on owners of diseased animals. The extent of the disturbance depends on such matters as quarantine regulations, success of control measures, and the public's state of mind and attitude toward the work.

It is obviously difficult to make exact statements as to the effect of the California outbreak on the business life of the State, but Carl C. Plehn, professor of finance in the University of California, has made an admirable study of this question. His views, as set forth in a paper on the subject, are essentially as follows:

As a result of the drought and of foot-and-mouth disease, two misfortunes whose effects are interwoven, there was a depression in business in California, beginning in March, 1924, and reaching its lowest point in June, amounting to a loss reaching, for June, to about 18 per cent in business in general. An analysis of all the facts seems to warrant the conclusion that the quarantine embargoes may fairly be chargeable with causing one-third of this depression, the other two-thirds being attributable to the drought and a few other local disturbances. The ill effects of the drought were intensified by the embargoes.

Naturally the most severe sufferers were the meat-products and dairy-products industries. Next in order came poultrymen and growers of early vegetables and fruits which were ready for market during the period of the embargoes. It was a great good fortune that the embargoes were relaxed before the great field crops and the bulk of the fruit and vegetable crops were ready for market.

Private losses, in addition to the general business losses and other than those assumed by the Federal, State, and county Governments, did not exceed $1,000,-000. The total of all ascertainable "out of pocket" expenses and losses, including the animals killed on account of exposure, was about $7,000,000.

Except for a part of the animals killed the losses were not capital losses, but income losses. It is bad enough to lose a part of a year's income, but that is not so bad as to lose one's capital and hence suffer an impairment of future income. California's capital wealth is in excess of $12,500,000,000, of which the value of all animals is about 1 per cent. The total of animals killed by the quarantine officers equaled about 2 per cent of all the animals and a large part of those so killed would have been slaughtered for meat the same year or next, thus representing income rather than capital. Without attempting to make the calculation exactly, it is safe to say that the capital loss was less than 0.02 per cent (two hundredths of 1 per cent) of the whole, a relatively very small amount. The two misfortunes of 1924 have therefore but slightly impaired the future of California and but slightly diminished her wealth.

RUMORS OF BUSINESS FAILURES

Rumors that a large number of small meat dealers failed in business during the drop in consumption of meat are not confirmed by figures relating to the number of bankruptcies and were absolutely untrue. One story was that 700 out of 1,000 small meat shops in Los Angeles failed. Undoubtedly a considerable number of these dealers lost a week's profits or more, but there seems to be no evidence beyond this temporary embarrassment that their business was seriously injured. In Merced County, however, according to a report by the farm adviser, "almost all the stores reported heavy losses in trade and from one-half to two-thirds of the clerks were laid off in some places."

UMEMPLOYMENT

As to unemployment in general, there is no evidence that foot-and-mouth disease caused any unemployment with the following exceptions: Men originally employed in caring for the animals killed were forced to find new jobs temporarily. The number so displaced did not exceed 2 per cent of all employees in charge of animals and those found new jobs until their old jobs were restored by restocking. In some localities retail stores laid off part of their staffs and real-estate agents were temporarily idle. In this connection between 4,000 and 5,000 men were temporarily employed as quarantine guards and as inspectors and the like.

PUREBRED BREEDING HERDS

Taking into consideration the closeness with which infection approached the registered purebred breeding herds in numerous localities it was the State's good fortune to keep the losses of such valuable animals down to a minimum. In fact, with the exception of scattered registered breeding bulls, the losses were confined practically to one breed—the Holstein-Friesian. And the losses within that breed were limited practically to four herds that contained females in numbers. Among these four, however, was one of the largest herds in the State, which was widely rated by competent judges as the greatest collection of high-class breeding cows anywhere existing in one unit. The total number of animals destroyed in this herd was 290. Perhaps the most noteworthy animal destroyed in this herd was the world-famous cow, Tilly Alcartra, the world's greatest, long-time producer. An important factor in connection with this herd was the owner's previous removal of all his heifers from the main herd. It was his practice to remove them when 6 months old to another farm 125 miles distant: at the time of slaughter of the main herd he had 138 heifers from 6 months to 2 years of age on this distant farm. They were never infected and consequently were saved.

EMBARGOES

As to embargoes, the most severe restrictions were those imposed by the three contiguous States and by Washington and Hawaii. In the case of Arizona the restrictions, in particular as to the movement of automobiles and of persons, were harshly enforced and were supported by a show of arms.

For a time Arizona closed all highways to travel from California, but these restrictions were later modified to permit travel subject to disinfection and fumigation requirements. These methods were considered of very doubtful value by experienced livestock sanitarians, and it is very probable that their maintenance was in many instances brought about by pressure of public opinion. In the case of Hawaii nearly all trade between San Francisco and Honolulu was suspended for many months.

POULTRY INDUSTRY

Poultry, presumably barnyard fowl, became contraband under practically all the quarantine embargoes. Until the plan of certifying clean products from clean districts became operative, no distinction was made between poultry from the cattle farms and those which had never been near any cattle. This imposed special hardship on such districts as Petaluma and parts of Merced, San Benito, and Los Angeles Counties, where the poultry industry is a large business.

TOURIST TRAVEL

During 1924 the aggregate travel to the Yosemite (used as a typical basis for comparison) totaled 105,894 persons as against 130,046 for 1923, a drop of 18 per cent. Of these, 73,718 came in automobiles in 1924, and this number is 16 per cent less than the 87,870 persons who came in their own cars the year before. Train travel declined 21 per cent. Of the two largest private resorts in the valley, one closed early, and they both ran far below capacity except over the Fourth of July. The public camps were less well filled than usual except for short periods.

The foot-and-mouth-disease embargoes discouraged travel, not only because of the actual discomforts resulting from the spraying of automobiles and disinfection of boots, camp outfits, and the like, but on account of the many tales spread abroad that the embargoes were more severe than they were. As a matter of fact, except for a short time, few roads were actually closed by the embargoes, but the atmosphere was one of uncertainty and mistrust.

SUMMARY OF ECONOMIC LOSSES

From the foregoing discussion it appears that the maximum depression of business, caused by foot-and-mouth disease, was about 6 per cent, that the meat-products, dairy, and poultry industries were the most severe sufferers, that total expenses and losses amounted to about $7,000,000, that the principal losses were losses of income, and that the capital loss was less than 0.02 (two hundredths of 1 per cent).

Rumors of business failures were greatly exaggerated. With rare exceptions the outbreak was not a cause of unemployment, and only a few purebred breeding herds became infected. Ill-considered embargoes caused more interference with business than the disease itself, and reduction on tourist travel was due to uncertainty and distrust rather than to the closing of roads or actual inconvenience.

A California paper voiced essentially the same conclusion by the following editorial discussion:

Seen through the magnifying glass of fear and hysteria both in and out of the State, the hurt seemed immense. Seen in the light of cold fact, California's loss from this epidemic is negligible * * * When it is all over the cattlemen will probably have better stock than before and the State will look back on its alarms with a good deal of the feeling of the man who found he had been running from a rabbit instead of a bear * * * The cattle can all be replaced promptly. Reimbursement for the stock destroyed provides individual owners with the means.

STEPS TO PREVENT FUTURE OUTBREAKS

The question of garbage disposal from ships in port has been one of interest in connection with the introduction of foot-and-mouth disease into this country. The State law of California appears to be adequate to prohibit infection from ships' garbage, so far as the dumping of garbage into coastal waters is concerned. Briefly, the State law provides that garbage, carcasses of animals, refuse of slaughterhouse offal, etc., shall not be dumped or deposited in or on any navigable waters of the State or of the Pacific Ocean within 20 miles of the coast line of the State. It is a misdemeanor for boats loaded with such material to leave any point within the State without carrying an inspector appointed by the State board of health to enforce the provisions of this section of the law.

To cooperate with the United States Department of Agriculture in preventing the introduction of animal and vegetable infections, the Navy Department, on September 10, 1924, issued an order directing commandants of all naval districts concerning the manner in which garbage from naval vessels shall be disposed of. The order also became a part of navy-yard regulations. Its text is as follows:

(a) In order to prevent possibility of introduction of hoof-and-mouth disease, garbage from ships making port from any part of the world, except Canada, Mexico, Central America, and the West Indies, will be placed in barrels especially marked with broad red band. All such garbage will be burned. This garbage will be handled by the Public Works Department and will not be subject to disposal by outside contract. This disposition of garbage shall continue as long as foods from restricted ports remain on board. Commanding officers of ships involved will take measures to prevent conveyance ashore of fresh food products in any form.

(*b*) No ruminants (goats, lambs, etc.) or swine of any kind whatsoever that may have been taken on board from any place outside United States shall be permitted to land.

Several States also have issued regulations embodying the precautions contained in the foregoing order.

SPECIAL PROBLEMS ENCOUNTERED

Other steps which have been taken include control over the importation of used empty bags and bagging material, prohibition against the importation of cattle, sheep, other ruminants, or swine as ships' stores, and prohibition against the importation of fresh meats from regions in which foot-and-mouth disease or rinderpest exists. These measures were adopted through the promulgation of Amendments 3 and 6 to B. A. I. Order 286, Amendment 2 to B. A. I. Order 281, and B. A. I. Order 298.

Besides conducting the regular administrative and field work, officials in charge of eradicating foot-and-mouth disease encountered many special problems. Several of these problems are noteworthy because of the possibility of their recurring in the future.

Only two institutions in the State of California manufacture and distribute biological products. Investigation showed that these institutions did not import or distribute any foreign biological products during the year previous to the outbreak of foot-and-mouth disease.

When foot-and-mouth disease was discovered by the bay district one laboratory in the quarantined area had on hand 399,073 cubic centimeters of anti-hog-cholera serum, which was destroyed under Government supervision August 1, 1924.

During the 1914 outbreak of foot-and-mouth disease, biological products proved to be a means of spreading the disease. Therefore, special precautions were taken to prevent this in the 1924 outbreak.

The first problem of trench digging and the burying of infected herds occurred in the bay district in the vicinity of Oakland. It was necessary to find a suitable place for the trenches and to prepare them for about 25 herds comprising about 3,550 cattle, 8,300 hogs, and also a smaller number of sheep and goats. The infected premises extended over a distance of about 25 miles. Accordingly all available steam shovels, nine in number, in the vicinity of Oakland were procured.

A troublesome difficulty was the fact that the contracting companies did not realize that speed was required instead of precision. Most of the operators were more particular about making the trench neat and symmetrical, instead of merely a hole in which to bury livestock. But finally, by persistence in pointing out the importance of speed, this difficulty was overcome and the trenches were dug rapidly.

Difficulty was experienced also in hiring marksmen expert in killing livestock in trenches. In this part of the work the ability to learn the vital spot and hit it is highly important for humane reasons, for economy of ammunition, and for speed in completing eradication work. The solution to this problem lies in the very careful selection of men for firing squads.

Some difficulty also was experienced in keeping curious persons away from the scene of killing. One infected dairy of 51 cattle was well within the city limits of Oakland and the approach of the killing time naturally attracted a large number of curiosity seekers who wanted to witness the slaughter. It was necessary in this case to call on the city of Oakland to furnish special police to assist the regular guard in keeping the crowd away from the infected premises. The police closed the street until the animals were buried.

STRATEGY IN DEALING WITH DISEASE

In several respects the contagion of foot-and-mouth disease is like a fire and a method of "back firing" during the outbreak produced excellent results. Early in the outbreak the Pinole Valley district was a source of danger to surrounding areas and it was decided to kill the exposed as well as the infected herds. The back-fire process consisted in driving cattle down from both slopes of the valley to the various trenches, where they were slaughtered. The trenches were necessarily very large. The method cleared the hills of exposed cattle and prevented the possible spread of infection through stray animals. The back fire checked the further spread of the disease.

As another example of special problem, difficulties caused by alkali water in the boilers of steam shovels may be mentioned. The water in the vicinity of Rodeo, Calif., is highly charged with alkali and when used in boilers caused excessive foaming, springing down of the crown sheet, leaking in the flues, and the necessity of having boilermakers from San Francisco make repairs. To prevent further difficulty of that nature, water was trucked from the city of Richmond, a distance of 20 miles.

DIFFICULT PROBLEMS IN PUBLIC RELATIONS

One of the most troublesome annoyances to officials responsible for eradicating foot-and-mouth disease was the insistent demand to give alleged remedies a trial. Persons who made these demands were seldom familiar with the true nature of the disease nor with the research work that had been conducted on it abroad. When they failed to persuade State and Federal officials to depart from the tested methods of eradication by quarantine, slaughter, and disinfection, aggrieved persons sometimes induced the press to publish their contentions.

During the 1924 outbreak the Bureau of Animal Industry received hundreds of letters from all parts of the country, but mostly from the Western States, requesting authority for the writers to go to California to try out their ideas. Most of these people wanted pay for their "cures." The sum of $1,000,000 was the highest price asked, though only one had so much nerve. Many demanded that they be given $100,000 if their cures worked all right. The cheapest one heard from asked $10,000. A typical cure sent to the Washington office of the bureau proved to be merely sheep-dip solution colored pink with cochineal.

There was also a natural tendency among a few press writers to make the most of dramatic events and to exaggerate the conditions, thereby surrounding the work with a sensational atmosphere.

The following article from a national magazine is a sample of the exaggerated statements:

Meanwhile counties spared the infection promptly drew rigid quarantine lines against neighboring infected counties. Whole areas of suspected territory were laid under the grim sovereignty of poison squads, which laid bait to destroy all feathered and furred life therein. And Arizona planted machine guns at the eastern end of the bridge across the Colorado River to warn away a host of auto caravaners out of infected districts in California.

The sheriff of one county in California requested the governor to send State troops to patrol quarantined areas there. But learning of the request, the Federal inspector in charge pointed out that troops were not needed to maintain quarantine in the limited area involved.

Finally, the California press, sensing the serious consequences of sensational publicity, used its influence to restore confidence. As an example one editor urged:

It is time to call a halt on the senseless hysteria over the foot-and-mouth disease. This mad and baseless panic is threatening destruction and ruin to many lines of business and demoralization to human activity in southern California. It has practically stopped auto travel, tending to isolate communities and individuals, bankrupted some stock owners, paralyzed some ranches, crippled trade, and begotten disastrous embargoes by other States.

Various organizations were active, independently and through the State Department of Agriculture, in disseminating practical, useful information and in giving support to the work of eradication. Following are typical extracts from " Foot-and-Mouth Disease Facts," issued at the Sacramento headquarters with the approval of the officials engaged in suppressing the disease:

The Federal regulations provide that claims will not be allowed if it is determined that the owner has not complied with all quarantine regulations.

No compensation will be made in case livestock is infected as a result of negligence on the part of the owner.

It is more humane to slaughter a comparatively few infected and exposed animals and eradicate the disease in this manner, than to let it spread to ranges and permit a much larger number to die not only from disease but from starvation and thirst as well.

When milkers, employees, or owners leave or return to the premises they should change clothing and disinfect the hands and shoes in a strong solution of chloride of lime. If shoes are clean, a solution of 1 pound to 3 gallons is strong enough; if not, the solution should be very much stronger. It is better to use as much chloride of lime as can be dissolved in the water.

Every farmer and rancher having large herds of stock should immediately separate them into smaller herds. This should be done as an actual economic precaution; if one animal contracts foot-and-mouth disease in a herd of 5,000 sheep, goats, or cattle it is absolutely necessary, for the eradication of the disease, to slaughter the whole herd. If, however, such a herd were divided into smaller herds, the loss would be in direct proportion to the number of smaller herds into which the one large herd was divided.

Curiosity is one of the greatest menaces confronting those engaged in eradicating foot-and-mouth disease. It is not with malice or viciousness that farmers and their families and their hired help, also townspeople and tourists, flock to an infected district and even to an infected farm. (Fig. 11.) It is curiosity. Like anything that is new, people want to know about it, and it is very natural that on learning of an infected animal in their vicinity, people journey to see it. It is difficult to educate a community in a short time to the gravity of the situation, to let people know the grave danger of letting their curiosity lead them to the vicinity of an infected animal or premises.

Farm hands and milkers naturally wish to leave premises that are infected with foot-and-mouth disease, and they leave to find work in some far-distant quarter. The comparison has been drawn that farm hands leaving an infected premises can spread the disease as readily as they might scatter seeds in a field. Do not allow strangers or visitors to enter the premises except on the most urgent business. Likewise do not visit other dairy premises and above all do not visit premises known to be infected with foot-and-mouth disease. In case of urgent business, arrange for proper disinfection.

Do not attempt to shoot blackbirds or pigeons, as to do so causes them to scatter. The better plan is to give them poisoned grain on a raised platform or other manner that will prevent domestic fowls or animals from eating the grain. The grain is to be poisoned according to the following formula:

Dissolve 1 ounce of strychnine in 1 pint of hot water. Add a thick starch paste until the product equals 3 quarts of thin starch paste. This is sufficient when thoroughly stirred to coat 30 quarts of cracked corn or other grain. Spread to dry. When dry, scatter in places accessible to blackbirds and pigeons, but inaccessible to fowls or animals not to be poisoned; a raised platform is suggested. Greater success will be met if the birds are fed unpoisoned grain until they get accustomed to taking it freely. Use grain which is commonly eaten by the birds in the vicinity.

Fig. 11.—Quarantine signs, supplementing the guard system, warned the public against visiting "posted" premises. The text of this sign was : "This farm has been placed under protective quarantine. Trespassers, agents, peddlers, and others are warned to keep out. Violators will be prosecuted under act of June 3, 1921. J. P. Iverson, Division of Animal Industry." This form of quarantine was enforced by the State of California

The following discussion occurred at a public meeting in California while the campaign of eradication was in progress. It illustrates typical attitudes of residents toward measures to control the spread of the disease. Referring to a certain county which was alleged to have "invited the world to come to its rivers to fish," a resident demanded why his own county should keep its roads closed to its mountain streams. "Some people," a public-spirited resident replied to the question, "put a little pleasure above the welfare of this country, this State, and, if you please, the United States. If this disease spreads you will be lucky to have money to buy bait for fishing in the mountains. There will be no business in this State next year if this thing gets away from you. We are not fooling the rest of the States by soft pedaling this business—we are only pulling the wool over our own eyes." Voicing the same sentiment, a woman rose and stated simply that while she earned her livelihood through maintaining a summer resort in the mountains, she favored keeping the roads closed if by so doing the spread of the disease would be checked. (Fig. 12.)

THE TEXAS OUTBREAK, 1924

On September 27, 1924, an outbreak of foot-and-mouth disease in Texas was officially confirmed. Reports reaching the bureau on September 25 indicated the presence of the disease so plainly, however, that a force of employees experienced in handling such outbreaks was directed by wire to proceed at once to Houston, Tex. At the same time the department issued an order quarantining the counties of Harris and Galveston, and those portions of Fort Bend and Brazoria Counties east of the Brazos River.

FIG. 12.—Closing roads in the quarantined area was necessary at times to check the spread of disease. However, the officials in charge of eradicating the outbreak planned the work so as to interfere as little as possible with the normal traffic and business activities of the State. The Federal and State officials closed roads only in the seriously infected localities

The infection first appeared in a herd of Zebu cattle south of Houston. J. E. Boog-Scott, chairman of the Texas Livestock Sanitary Commission, and L. G. Cloud, State veterinarian, proceeded immediately to that point and took charge of the State employees assigned to the work. On October 1, at the request of the governor of Texas, the United States Department of Agriculture assumed full charge of the eradication work in that State, the combined forces being under the direction of Marion Imes, of the Bureau of Animal Industry.

The duration of this outbreak was just 30 days, only 11 herds becoming infected, though, as later discussed, a very unusual recurrence appeared some months afterwards. Following a thorough investigation, there appeared to be no evidence that the Texas outbreak was in any way connected with the one in California, approximately 2,000 miles distant.

PROBABLE ORIGIN OF INFECTION

The disease first appeared in a pasture on a ranch about 20 miles from Houston, on the Galveston-Houston highway, and spread to other pastures on the ranch and to neighboring cattle. Among the possible sources of infection investigated the most probable was visits to the pasture by sailors or stevedores coming from infected countries. The originally infected ranch borders a much-traveled highway. Water is supplied to the pastures from wells by. means of windmills. There is a windmill, an elevated storage tank, and a circular iron watering tank in the pasture where the disease first appeared. This water-supply system is in plain view from the highway and about 600 feet from it. As evidence that the water system is visited by a large number of the men who tramp the highway, there is a beaten path from the road to the water tank. It was not uncommon for such persons to bathe in the tank or to wash some of their clothing soiled while aboard ship.

Numerous other sources of possible infection, especially merchandise from South America, were investigated but without the plausible evidence in the case just mentioned. It is a common practice for Spanish and also British ships with Hindu crews to carry live animals as ship stores. A few French and Italian ships have also followed the same practice. The animals are bought at any port where they are available. They are kept on board and are slaughtered as fresh meat is required. Cattle, sheep, goats, and sometimes hogs are carried in this way and they do not appear on the ship's manifests except as ship stores. It is reasonable to believe that some of these animals may have been picked up in countries in which foot-and-mouth disease exists and that some of them were exposed to the disease. Such being the case there would be danger that the infection was carried ashore by sailors and also by stevedores when the ship landed at a later port.

The cattle ranch, as mentioned, is on the Galveston-Houston highway, about 20 miles southeast of Houston. On September 12 the owner noticed that some of the cattle were sick and the following day called a local practitioner. Not being certain of the diagnosis, the veterinarian visited the herd again Sunday, September 14. Fully 12 cattle showed lesions at that time. Suspecting foot-and-mouth disease, the veterinarian reported the case by long-distance telephone to the State veterinarian. The Bureau of Animal Industry inspector at Houston also was notified. Inoculation tests confirmed the first suspicions. The State and bureau representatives took every precaution to prevent the spread of the disease. Local quarantines were declared and guards stationed to enforce them. Work on a burial trench began promptly. Doctor Cole handled the bureau work efficiently until September 28, when Doctor Imes arrived from California to take charge.

On September 26 foot-and-mouth disease was discovered among cattle in an adjoining pasture on another ranch. Unfortunately the owner had cut 50 stray cattle that mingled with his herd and turned them out on the open range the day before visible lesions appeared in his own cattle. These strays were directly exposed and they probably would have spread the infection throughout the area; but all range cattle with which they mingled were gathered and slaughtered before the disease had time to develop.

Small herds in fenced inclosures were not taken in the round-up; but as the disease began to develop in such herds in different parts of the area all remaining cloven-footed animals in the exposed area were purchased and slaughtered. This seemingly drastic action was taken only after the most careful consideration and because of the peculiar local conditions which necessitated prompt and effective measures to prevent a general outbreak over the coastal plains country.

LIMITED EXTENT OF OUTBREAK

The infection was confined to the original area and the disease was eradicated within 30 days from the time the field forces got into action. Relations with the press were handled direct by the headquarters office and were maintained on a cordial basis of cooperation.

A new departure was made in handling relations with common carriers. The district manager of the American Railway Association arranged with the various railway companies for the formation of a railway quarantine bureau. The quarantine bureau maintained an office adjoining the bureau and State offices.

METHOD OF ERADICATION

INSPECTIONS

The customary systematic inspections were made of all susceptible animals in the exposed area and surrounding country. In addition, there were numerous calls for inspection outside the quarantined area. The inspection force encouraged owners to report any suspected cases and all calls were answered promptly. This took much of the time of the inspectors. Because of the wide drifting of cattle and the constant mingling of herds it was deemed necessary to conduct systematic inspections over more territory than is usually included around the infected area.

DISPOSAL OF CARCASSES

In planning the disposal work in Harris County a corral and crowding chutes were constructed while the first trenches were being dug. Equipment known as a drag-line outfit was used, on account of the heavy, sticky clay encountered, in which ordinary steamshovel equipment can not work successfully. As soon as the first trench was completed, the drag-line equipment started another trench while the slaughtering operations were under way in the first one. The trenches radiated from the corral, somewhat like spokes of a wheel from the hub. This plan enabled the slaughtering and trenching crews to work at the same time and saved moving the corrals and chutes.

In Galveston County a different method of disposal was used. Because of delay in obtaining digging equipment and also because of the expected approach of a rainy season, which would seriously interfere with digging, arrangements were made to incinerate the infected animals. To accomplish this, short pieces of railroad rails were placed across a drainage ditch about 18 inches from the bottom. Full-length rails were then placed across the short ones and cordwood piled on. The animals were driven into a temporary corral surrounding the site, slaughtered, and dragged on to the rails by tractors. Fuel oil was then poured over the mass and lighted. As the ·bottom of the ditch was not level, oil flowed toward one end where a dirt dam checked it. The carcasses were completely consumed and the incineration was considered a success. Each disposal site had its disinfecting station through which all persons were required to enter and leave. Gas-tight chests provided means for fumigating all clothing which needed such treatment.

Cleaning and disinfecting operations included the cleaning and disinfecting of premises, stock cars, stockyards and packing-house yards, dipping of hides, fumigating of wool and other commodities, operations of disinfecting stations, and movement of hay and manure. All these lines were under one control because they are closely related, and idle men could be shifted from one line to another to meet sudden demands. After premises were cleaned and disinfected in the regular manner, the pastures and ranges were burned. This was done by first burning around buildings and structures with flame throwers and then lighting the grass by dragging across the range a burning sack soaked in oil. Mounted men usually dragged these sacks. The cleaning and disinfecting work included all railroad yards and chutes in and around the infected area.

DAIRY AND CREAMERY WORK

The dairy and creamery work was handled in the usual manner and details changed only to meet local conditions. Raw milk produced in the exposed area was allowed to be transported only to an approved pasteurizing plant. One inspector devoted all his time to supervising establishments that fed garbage to hogs. None of the garbage-fed hogs contracted the disease.

GUARDS

At least one guard was stationed at each infected place, and in some cases it was necessary to have two guard posts. Line riders also were employed. The Texas ranger force, exercising the police powers of the State, was a part of the consolidated foot-and-mouth-disease organization. The Texas and the Southwest Cattle Raisers' Association furnished brand inspectors, and cooperated in other ways. The United States Biological Survey furnished two men trained in the control of predatory animals. County extension agents, under the direction of the director of extension of the agricultural college, certified to shipments of farm products from the free area.

TABLE 2.—*Summary of slaughter and appraisal, Texas, 1924*

	Herd	Animals slaughtered				Appraised value
		Cattle	Sheep	Hogs	Total	
Harris County	145	8, 212	0	69	8, 281	$315, 093. 50
Galveston County	3	261	27	0	288	9, 847. 00
	148	8, 473	27	69	8, 569	324, 940. 50
Infected	11	3, 125	27	11	3, 163	
Exposed	137	5, 348	0	58	5, 406	
Property destroyed						158. 86
Total	148	8, 473	27	69	8, 569	325, 099. 36

DISEASE RECURS IN TEXAS

On July 26, 1925, foot-and-mouth disease again appeared in Texas after its apparent suppression the previous year. The recurrence occurred in Harris County a few miles south of Houston in a herd of Zebu cattle owned by W. S. Jacobs, whose cattle were the first to be infected in the outbreak of the previous year.

Immediately on observing the symptoms of the disease the owner reported his suspicions to the Bureau of Animal Industry inspector at Houston, Tex., who inspected the cattle the following day, telegraphed the Washington office of the bureau, and inoculated test animals. T. W. Cole, of the Federal forces, and N. F. Williams, State veterinarian, arrived in Houston July 28 and after inspecting the cattle, quarantined the premises, placed them under guard, and prepared for the slaughter and disposal of the diseased herd.

EXTENT OF OUTBREAK

All cattle in the vicinity were inspected as rapidly as the limited number of inspectors could cover the area. No other infection was found until August 5, when a small herd of dairy cattle grazing on the open range between South Houston and Pasadena, Tex., showed the presence of the disease.

A rapid survey demonstrated that approximately 5,000 range cattle were exposed, some of them showing infection. A force of experienced veterinary inspectors, mounted and accompanied by one or more riders familiar with the range, cut out all animals showing suspicious symptoms. These animals were combined with the infected dairy herd and the entire lot slaughtered August 6. The carcasses were destroyed by incineration.

On August 25 additional infection was found on the open range north of the Houston ship channel, about 4 miles from the infected area near Pasadena. This channel extends in a westerly direction from Galveston Bay to Houston, about 25 miles. The last 16 miles pass through a range and farming country, and cattle graze to the water line on both sides of the channel, even around the docks. The infection is believed to have been carried by a bull moved from the infected Pasadena area in violation of quarantine.

Since the area north of the ship channel bordered an immense open-range country in which disease-control operations would be very difficult, about 19 miles of woven-wire fence was constructed. This fence was hog-tight and for emergency reasons was completed in three and one-half days. Most of the hogs in the region were half wild. All susceptible animals within the area inclosed by the fences were slaughtered.

On September 4 the first case of foot-and-mouth disease was detected in Galveston County, which adjoins Harris County. The infection probably was accidentally carried by persons from the area around South Houston. Court injunctions applied for by local interests delayed disposal of infected cattle in Galveston County and the disease spread over a considerable area before it was finally eradicated. The last infected herd in this area was disposed of October 2.

On September 8 a dairy herd in Harrisburg, a suburb of Houston, was found to be infected. Harrisburg is a separate corporation but adjoins Houston and the two are one continuous city. The owner of the herd retailed raw milk in the vicinity and the dairy was in a thickly settled community. When discovered, the disease was well advanced. Several other dairies were near the infected premises. A prompt survey showed that cattle belonging to two neighbors were infected. These animals were killed and burned as well as cattle that were in direct contact with the infection. On September 15 cattle on premises a mile south of the dairy first infected developed the disease. These and contact cattle were killed and burned the same day. Three other cows, found to be infected September 20, were killed and burned the same day. Daily inspections were made throughout the district and in the outlying territory inspectors examined the stock every two or three days. All condemned cattle in this district were destroyed by burning, and disinfection was started on all infected premises the same day the cattle were destroyed. The infection in this district probably was carried there by the owner of the Harrisburg herd, who owned property near South Houston and visited cattlemen and dairymen there frequently.

The next case occurred September 15 between Park Place and South Houston. The infection appeared to have come from the Harrisburg area.

On October 2 infection of foot-and-mouth disease was found in range cattle 2 miles west of Webster, Tex. This outbreak was quickly eradicated and outside of the round-up area there was only one case traceable to this area of infection. This single case appeared October 14 in a dairy herd one-half mile from Webster. The infected animal was burned within a few hours and all exposed animals were disposed of the following day. This was the last case of foot-and-mouth disease in the State.

Infection during the 1925 outbreak was confined to comparatively small areas in Harris and Galveston Counties. Both of these counties were quarantined and also the portion of Brazoria County east of the Brazos River. The borders of the " closed area " were extended as the disease spread, but the area at all times was kept as small as was consistent with safety.

The work was conducted on a cooperative basis with the Texas Livestock Sanitary Commission, until September 23, 1925, when, at the request of the governor, Doctor Imes of the Bureau of Animal Industry assumed full direction of the campaign.

The plan used in 1924 under which the American Railway Association detailed a representative to organize and handle railway, steamship, and express business was again put into effect. Truck lines were added to the other common carriers in 1925 and the permit business was greatly simplified.

All expenses of eradication work in Texas, except salaries and travel accounts of regular employees, and minor items, such as office expense, were shared equally by the Federal Bureau of Animal Industry and the State of Texas.

METHOD OF ERADICATION

QUARANTINE AND INSPECTION MEASURES

As in former outbreaks, the customary methods of quarantine and inspection were used. Daily inspections were made of susceptible animals in the exposed area. In adjoining areas inspections were made usually about every other day and in some cases once in three days. Because of the wide drifting of cattle and constant mingling of herds, inspections were extended over more territory than is common around infected areas. Calls for inspections within and outside the quarantined area of cases suspected by owners were numerous, and all were answered promptly.

In making range inspections round-up outfits were used. Each outfit consisted of experienced cowboys, saddle horses, chuck wagon, a cook, and a truck for hauling dead and crippled animals from the range. A ranger who lived in the closed area usually was hired as "boss rider" and was instructed to assemble a round-up crew of riders familiar with the wooded country and to gather all open-range cattle. A camp was provided where the riders stayed while the work lasted, no one leaving the infected district. The cattle were rounded up, all brands being recorded in a brand book. Two appraisers, Federal and State, appraised them, after which they were put into holding pens ready for slaughter. Meanwhile other groups of riders were searching the woods and bringing all cattle from all directions. With this system there was no loss of time and the work was continued early and late until the range was cleared of cattle.

All wagons, trucks, automobiles, and other conveyances were sprayed with a disinfectant on leaving the " closed area."

The infected area in Harris County consisted of large, open prairie for the central part, surrounded by dense woods and traversed by many gulleys and two small bayous. The area included several small towns in which cattle ran freely in the streets and among the buildings. Town cows and range cattle mingled together, the former often ranging 2 miles or more from the towns where they belonged. In the northern and western part of the area there were several dairies, the cattle of which ran on open range.

The guards employed during the outbreak worked in two shifts of 12 hours each. Their duties were light, mainly to prevent livestock from drifting along highways, and also that of inspecting wagons and trucks to prevent the transportation of forbidden commodities. Arrangements were made through the area coordinator for the use of 40 Army tents for use by the guards. These were used throughout the campaign, thus saving the cost of new equipment. The guards were under a captain and three lieutenants, the captain being a member of the central organization and the lieutenants local men selected for ability and trustworthiness.

Inspections extended also to merchandise offered by business houses for shipment out of the infected or exposed areas. The railroad and express companies would not receive shipments without permits from State or Federal inspectors.

Following the report, on September 3, of a suspicious herd of cattle thought to be affected with foot-and-mouth disease,.near Arcadia, in Galveston County, guard lines were at once established. Mounted patrols were placed on the outside of pastures involved, and all highways and railroad crossings along the lines were closed and guarded.

By September 15 practically all cattle, sheep, and goats were disposed of, though a few strays were later found by riders who rode through the ·woods for that purpose. About 250 wild range hogs were in the woods and along the ship channel. Many of them could not be driven and had to be shot when found. Most of them were gathered by mounted men with trained hog dogs, driven to pens built in the woods, appraised, earmarks taken, and burned. This work was practically finished in five days. It is noteworthy that of about 250 hogs on the same range where infection in cattle was plentiful only 6 hogs showed lesions of foot-and-mouth, disease.

SUPERVISION OF CREAMERIES, DAIRIES, AND GARBAGE FEEDING

Producers of raw milk in the closed area were required to take out permits, and such permits were issued for the transportation of raw milk to Pasteurizing plants only. Most of the creameries located in Houston and Galveston and all creameries and vehicles handling milk from the closed area were kept under close supervision to prevent spread of the disease through these channels.

Many hog feeders about Houston feed garbage. Other cities in the quarantined territory have smaller numbers of such hog feeders. All garbage-feeding establishments were placed and kept under supervision, the work being handled in the usual manner. No foot-and-mouth disease appeared in any of the garbage-fed hogs.

DISPOSAL OF CARCASSES

Two methods of carcass disposal were followed throughout the campaign of eradication: (1) Destruction by incineration, and (2) the usual trench burial. The former method has solved the problem of dangerous delays experienced while waiting for trench space.

DISPOSAL BY INCINERATION

In the 1924 outbreak experimental work on methods of burning carcasses received considerable attention, and in 1925 this branch of foot-and-mouth-disease eradication received added study. The disposal force consisted of four crews with a lay inspector in charge of each. Each incinerating unit was equipped with an engine and two oil burners with all necessary equipment, including a moderate supply of fuel, all mounted on a light, speedy truck.

Except in cases of extensive infection, where all the incinerating units were needed, one unit usually was held in reserve at headquarters to answer sudden calls. In this way prompt action was possible in new areas. Within a few minutes after notice of a " break " was received by telephone the crew was assembled and the truck was on the way. In the case of new infection reported late in the day shifts were arranged so that burning work could proceed without interruption 24 hours a day, until all the animals to be. disposed of were burned or a trench was ready.

The machines used for burning were well adapted for outdoor work, produced an intensely hot flame, and proved to be satisfactory. The burners atomized almost any kind of fuel from distillate to heavy crude oil and stood the rough usage of field work. About 1,300 animals were destroyed by incineration.

When burning of carcasses is properly conducted it has no seriously objectionable features. In one locality, where in the course of four days 174 animals were incinerated, the seat of operation was virtually surrounded by residence property. Though the inspectors made numerous inquiries afterwards, not a complaint was received with reference to objectionable odors or other features encountered.

Compared with disposal of carcasses by burial, incineration was a considerably more rapid method, except where large herds were involved.

On October 14 foot-and-mouth disease appeared 1½ miles east of Webster, Tex. Forty minutes after confirmation was established, the infected animal had been killed and was being incinerated, and in 24 hours the entire herd in which the infection had occurred was burned. No infection was found in the herd other than the one animal. Within 48 hours from the time the first infection was discovered all contact cattle had been burned. In all, 267 cattle were destroyed in this locality and the spread of the disease was immediately stopped. Trenching machinery could not have been used since water saturated the ground and the pit would have been filled with water as fast as it was dug. A strong wind aids in the disposal of carcasses by incineration and reduces the quantity of oil necessary. In one instance, when a strong wind aided the work, the destruction of 134 cattle required only 15 barrels of crude oil, which is less than half the usual quantity needed.

The advantages of incineration are briefly as follows: It is a quick disposal, thereby preventing disease from spreading. It requires little space, and has been conducted on an ordinary-sized city lot. It does not mar topography or landscape. There are no objectionable odors to combat, either before or after. The use of lime is eliminated. Incineration creates a favorable impression on the public. Table 3 presents the quantity of fuel needed for the destruction of varying numbers of mature cattle of average size.

TABLE 3.—*Fuel required to destroy completely varying numbers of cattle*

Number of cattle	Ground dimensions of pyre	Fuel		Number of cattle	Ground dimensions of pyre	Fuel	
		Oak wood	Oil			Oak wood	Oil
	Feet	*Cords*	*Barrels*		*Feet*	*Cords*	*Barrels*
5	8 by 8	2	2	35	12 by 24	9	12
10	8 by 12	3	4	50	12 by 28	10	15
15	8 by 16	4	5	75	12 by 36	13	25
25	8 by 20	7	8	100	16 by 44	18	30

A moderate number of calves, hogs, and sheep can be fitted into the spaces among the cattle.

As to materials found most satisfactory, hardwood, principally oak in 4-foot lengths, is especially desirable and the figures are based on that kind of wood. For the first two or three layers of the pyre green wood is somewhat better adapted for the work than well-seasoned wood, since it does not burn so rapidly and holds the carcasses off the ground longer, thereby making possible a current of air underneath.

" Pipe-line " crude oil that is not too heavy works well through the burners and is somewhat better adapted for the work than distillate, though this also proved to be satisfactory. Also, the crude oil is generally somewhat cheaper than distillate. Fleshy parts of carcasses are consumed within a few hours and the remainder at the end of about 15 hours.

In connection with destruction of infected animals by burning, experience has shown that incinerating a single carcass, especially of a large animal such as a bull, requires an excessive quantity of fuel by comparison with the proportional quantity for incinerating a larger number. In some instances wood was used as the only fuel. A herd of eight cattle and one hog, all of which were infected, was destroyed by burning on a pyre built of logs and other available wood. There was no cost for fuel in this case except the item of labor. Decision as to the kind or combination of fuels naturally depends on their availability and relative prices when purchase is necessary.

CONSTRUCTION OF TRENCHES

Trench burial of carcasses was handled in a manner similar to that used in 1924 in Texas when the system of having a single, long trench was abandoned in favor of a series of shorter trenches somewhat like the spokes from the hub of a wheel, radiating from a central chute. In this method two steam shovels are necessary to keep the work moving rapidly. One is kept excavating while the other is used as a crane for placing the carcasses and covering them. There were five of these trench sites, three in Harris and two in Galveston counties. Drag-line equipment was used for digging trenches.

In the combination of burning and burying as a means of disposing of infected stock lies much of the success in suppressing promptly the 1925 outbreak of the disease. The burning crews disposed of infected cattle, hogs, and other susceptible stock from the start, so that when pits were ready very little, if any, actual infection was left to come into the trenches. Incineration appeared to fill the long need for quicker action than has been possible in other foot-and-mouth-disease outbreaks.

A test of the trenching machinery showed that to dig trench room for 1,000 cattle required 20 hours' steady run of a drag-line outfit. In one instance trench-digging equipment was moved to a railroad switch near an infected pasture and held on a sidetrack in readiness for any possible spread. The outfit, however, was not unloaded, since burning crews were able to handle the situation satisfactorily.

CLEANING AND DISINFECTING OPERATIONS

Cleaning and disinfecting operations included the cleaning and disinfection of premises, stockyards, railroad stock pens, and other establishments. This activity included also fumigation of wool and pelts, disinfection of hides, handling of contaminated forage and manure, and the operation of disinfection stations.

The major part of the work was the cleaning and disinfecting of 562 premises from which infected and contact cattle had been taken in Harris, Galveston, and Brazoria Counties. Other work of the same unit was the disinfecting and fumigating of stockyards and railroad cars, and of about 150,000 hides in packing plants and hide houses. The work included also the disinfection and fumigation of about 300 business premises, such as burlap-bag houses and hay-and-grain houses, and disinfection of horses, mules, dogs, cats, poultry, and machinery used in various business enterprises. Another of the activities was the removal and burning of 746 tons of hay cut in pastures where infected cattle had been found.

Disinfecting tents were maintained at the various trenches. Each tent was divided by a railing, with gate, into two sections, "clean" and "infected." On entering the tent, workers removed clean clothing and left it on the clean side. The men then passed to the infected side and were furnished with clothing to wear in the trenches and infected territory. On returning, the men removed the clothing worn in infected regions, leaving it on the infected side of the tent. They then passed to the clean side and put on clothing worn on entering. Clothes worn in infected territory were disinfected, dried, and sent to be laundered.

Employees trained in cleaning and disinfection work were furnished to power, light, telephone, and oil companies to look after crews engaged in repair work in infected territory. Arrangements were made with the various companies to furnish extra clothing to the crews, such as overalls, jackets, and boots. On leaving infected areas the men exchanged their clothing for clean garments. Boots were disinfected. Crews washed hands in bichloride solution. Trucks going from an infected to a clean area were sprayed both inside and out.

Employees in the disinfection unit were utilized also in building fences, supervising disinfection of vehicles at guard stations, and in some cases in the incineration of carcasses. Methods at the disinfecting stations, at trench sites, and riders' camps were improved and systematized, making possible the performance of a great deal of work in a highly efficient manner.

TESTING AND RESTOCKING PREMISES

The infected open ranges and premises were kept free of livestock for 90 days. Mounted men patrolled the borders of infected areas constantly to keep susceptible animals away and to pick up any cattle, horses, and mules found on the range.

Beginning early in December, test herds were placed on individual premises and various ranges. Each herd on the ranges was in the care of a veterinarian and several riders and was inspected daily for 30 days. The riders directed the movement of the herds to various parts of the range so that all parts would be covered. Once each week the range test herds were carefully examined in a chute for foot-and-mouth lesions. The cattle used in test herds on the ranges were borrowed from friendly cattlemen, and those used for testing individual premises were furnished by owners of the premises.

On January 5, 1926, a test herd of 146 borrowed cattle was placed, with a veterinarian in charge and two riders, on the last range to be tested. The cattle were inspected daily and put through a chute for close inspection weekly for 30 days. With the exception of three cattle which died from the effects of a storm, all the remaining ones were returned to their owners in better condition than when received, the owners expressing satisfaction over this result. Results of the test showed no latent foot-and-mouth-disease virus present on any of the ranges or individual premises previously involved.

Following the testing of the ranges and individual premises, restocking gradually took place. After a period of continued inspection to make certain that no virus remained after the last case on October 14, 1925, all Federal quarantine restrictions imposed because of foot-and-mouth disease in the State were revoked, effective April 1, 1926.

SPECIAL DIFFICULTIES AND PROBLEMS

The harvesting and shipping of native or wild hay is an important industry in Harris, Galveston, and Brazoria Counties. Since livestock roam at will and few, if any, of the so-called hay lands are free from cattle, it was necessary to supervise the harvesting and shipping of hay from the quarantined territory.

Some of the local hay interests obtained an injunction against such interference in September, 1925. No hay was actually shipped, because the common carriers were not parties to the suit and they refused to move the hay; but various States, especially those near Texas, amended their orders and imposed drastic restrictions against Texas commerce. The work in Galveston and Brazoria Counties was seriously hampered and delayed by the injunctions, and not until after they were dissolved was the work resumed on the usual basis.

Most of the quarantine orders issued by other States against Texas were reasonable, and there was little interference with commerce from safe areas.

Within the State, cooperation of officials and organizations was excellent; but there was some opposition by individual stock owners and others in Galveston and Brazoria Counties and to a lesser extent in Harris County, who were opposed to eradication work. They did not believe there was foot-and-mouth disease in their locality or in the State, but thought that the disease was simply an aggravated form of a malady with which they were already familiar. Since all infected animals were burned and disposed of within a short time after visible lesions appeared, the owners had slight opportunity to see advanced cases. In one instance the owner of infected cattle gathered from the range would not consent to slaughter until unmistakable symptoms of foot-and-mouth disease appeared. The symptoms, however, developed the following day.

Stubborn resistance was often met in purchasing cattle for slaughter, small owners giving the most trouble. Much valuable time was lost in explaining to them the necessity of giving up their stock to prevent further spread of foot-and-mouth disease.

The inspectors engaged in both the California and Texas outbreaks deserve special commendation for their faithful work. Many of those detailed to Texas had been accustomed to high altitudes and suffered severely from the extreme summer heat at almost sea level while dressed in rubber. The force also endured misery from mosquitoes of extremely large size which were in the grass and other vegetation over which it was necessary to travel while making inspections. At times torrential rains added to difficulties of travel.

To haul fuel and equipment to certain premises, it was necessary to have tractors await the arrival of wood, oil, and supply trucks at points where they could not proceed under their own power and tow them one at a time to infected premises. Yet delays were surprisingly short even considering the condition of the roads. In one instance where the disease was reported at 11:30 a. m., cordwood, crude oil, and distillate arrived by means of tractor power within two hours, and incineration of the infected cattle was in progress before and during the night.

TRACING OF INFECTION

Extended investigation has failed to show definitely the source of the virus of foot-and-mouth disease, which evidently lived over from the previous year. The most probable explanation is (1) that the infection came from a surface pond in the pasture where the first symptoms appeared, or (2) that the infection was propagated by cattle ticks. The history of the first-infected herd in the 1925 recurrence of the disease is almost identical with that of the 1924 outbreak. The herd was owned by the same man, W. S. Jacobs, and the cattle grazed on the same pasture, which is in Harris County, south of Houston, Tex. The first symptoms of the 1925 infection appeared July 26, which was 283 days from the time the last infected animal in that region was disposed of in 1924. This is an unusually long time for the virus to live, but in Winton, Merced County, Calif., it remained alive for 345 days. Test cattle had been introduced into Doctor Jacobs's pasture and remained healthy until removed from the pastures, March 25, 1925. Moreover, the pond suspected as a possible source of the outbreak had been disinfected with chloride of lime in 1924 and again early in 1925. These facts gave support to the theory that southern fever ticks which infest that region may have carried the infection over from the previous year.

Investigations conducted by the writer demonstrated that the blood in the stomachs of adult ticks taken from acutely infected cattle actually carried the virus of foot-and-mouth disease to the inoculated guinea pigs. Tests made with seed ticks or progeny of infected ticks, however, were negative, which tends to disprove the tick hypothesis, as the virus would have to be carried by seed ticks if propagated by infected adult ticks of the preceding October.

The foregoing information illustrates the baffling nature of foot-and-mouth disease on which research is now being conducted by three American scientists, including one representative of the department, in Europe, where the disease is constantly present.

A study of the probable means by which infection spread from the first herd reveals that contact with range cattle was by far the most important cause. Of 153 cases investigated, infection was traced to range cattle in 142 instances. The few remaining cases were spread by dairy cattle owners, or unknown causes

Table 4 shows the appraised value of livestock and property destroyed and also the number of infected and exposed herds in the 1925 Texas outbreak:

TABLE 4.—*Number and value of infected and exposed livestock, Texas outbreak, 1925*

County	Herds		Cattle	Hogs	Sheep	Goats	Total number animals	Appraised value	Value of property destroyed
	Infected	Exposed							
Harris	96	629	12,314	630	811	342	14,097	$360,499.32	$10,544.00
Galveston	57	201	8,369	99	587	3	9,058	288,543.96	512.70
Brazoria	0	18	167	23	4	0	194	5,314.50	0
Total	153	848	20,850	752	1,402	345	23,349	654,357.78	11,056.70

MODE OF INFECTION STUDIED

Where the information was definite enough to be conclusive, new centers of infection in both the California and Texas outbreaks were traced generally to direct or indirect contact with infected animals and to human carriers. Other modes of infection played a minor rôle.

The fact that the feed was very short in many localities in California caused considerable straying and consequently more exposure among the herds of various owners. In one instance, in Pinole Valley of that State, one cow exposed a herd of 165 and another herd of 200 animals, with their consequent slaughter.

Table 5 shows in detail the probable manner in which the infection occurred in the California and Texas outbreaks. The figures are based on inspectors' reports following careful investigations:

TABLE 5.—*Herds slaughtered in California and Texas in which probable mode of infection was reported*

Mode of infection	California 1924	Texas		Total
		1924	1925	
Animals brought direct from infected public stockyards for slaughter, feeding, breeding, or dairy purposes	4			4
Animals brought from infected stables or lots of local dealers	3			3
Direct contact with neighboring infected herds by pasture, mating, breeding animals, or animals not confined	196	8	142	346
Infected railway cars	2			2
Persons visiting, exchanging work, stock buyers, peddlers, etc	67	2	5	74
Dogs, poultry, birds, etc	5			5
Infected public highways	16			16
Contaminated streams or drinking water	2			2
Infected feed or garbage	6			6
Other known sources of infection	7			7
Sources of infection unknown	79	1	6	86
	387	11	153	551

CONCLUSIONS BASED ON CALIFORNIA AND TEXAS OUTBREAKS

Advance preparation.—The outbreaks of 1902 and 1924 appeared in seaboard States, whereas those of 1908 and 1914 appeared first at inland points. Although it seems that territory surrounding ports of entry is more exposed, experience shows that future outbreaks may occur in any State of the Union. Realizing this and also the constant danger of invasions by other foreign diseases, the Bureau of Animal Industry, in May, 1917, in written communications urged the various States to provide funds or some other means of meeting their financial obligations in an emergency, also to pass adequate laws and promulgate suitable regulations, and to organize their veterinary forces so as to be able to act promptly in cooperation with the Federal Government in eradication work.

This matter was taken up with all the States by the bureau in 1917, and most of them approved the procedures, yet there are still many States not prepared with either adequate laws or sufficient funds should foot-and-mouth disease be discovered in them. The State constitution of California did not provide authority for paying indemnities for animals and other property destroyed on account of the disease; likewise the State of Texas had no funds for indemnifying the owners of slaughtered animals.

As a result, the cooperating authorities of both States were embarrassed and many of the stock owners who suffered loss of their animals were obliged to wait and trust to the next legislature to provide the authority and funds to meet the obligations of their State. The governors and other authorities of both States deserve much credit for the way they handled the difficult situation, and the bankers of those States deserve the gratitude of the livestock industry for the financial assistance they rendered. Advance preparation for the next outbreak, wherever it may occur, can not be urged too strongly.

Accurate diagnosis.—At the beginning of an outbreak before a definite diagnosis has been reached and sometimes during the prevalence of the disease, inoculation experiments must be made with susceptible animals in order to arrive at a prompt and accurate diagnosis.

Recent investigations have shown that guinea pigs are susceptible to vesicular stomatitis as well as to foot-and-mouth disease, and these are the two diseases which are the most difficult to differentiate. Therefore, guinea pigs should not be depended upon for establishing a diagnosis. Likewise, cattle and hogs may develop very similar lesions as the result of inoculation with foot-and-mouth disease and vesicular stomatitis, but they will not show such lesions if the disease is mycotic stomatitis. However, in the inoculation of horses we have a definite check, since these animals are very susceptible to vesicular stomatitis but have not been found to develop foot-and-mouth disease in any outbreak in this country. Therefore, it is desirable to inoculate at least two cattle, preferably between 1 and 2 years of age, two hogs, and two horses in any suspected outbreak. If vesicles already described occur in all three species of animals it is vesicular stomatitis, whereas if the cattle and hogs show these vesicles and the horses remain healthy, the diagnosis of foot-and-mouth disease is indicated. *Care should be taken, however, to obtain all these test animals from a community or from farms where neither of the diseases has prevailed. Mistakes have been made when apparently healthy animals obtained from the same farm where the suspected disease existed were inoculated, with negative results, only to find out later that they had previously suffered an attack of the disease and were therefore temporarily immune at the time of the injections.* In this connection the most recent lesions should be obtained and emulsified in the saliva of the suspected animal if obtainable; otherwise in a very small quantity of water that has been boiled and cooled. The mucous membrane of the lips, dental pads, and preferably the tongue of the horse, should be scarified and the suspected material rubbed into the abrasions. Intravenous inoculations are much less satisfactory, and feeding experiments should never be attempted. Although the virus of foot-and-mouth disease may exist in the blood and viscera in the early stages of the infection, such material should never be used. Vesicular fluid, denuded mucous membranes, and the necrotic (dead) tissues of erosions are always to be preferred in the order named.

Careful inspections.—The importance of carefully examining animals showing suspicious symptoms and continuing such examinations until it is definitely known whether the affection is foot-and-mouth disease, can not be emphasized too strongly. The failure of a local veterinarian in central California to recognize the disease in a herd of range cattle, although a number of the animals were lame and foot-and-mouth disease was known to exist in the State at that time, resulted in a tragedy to the livestock and business interests of the southern part of the State. His snap judgment of "gravel lameness" in this instance permitted exposed cattle to be shipped to the stockyards at Los Angeles, San Francisco, and Stockton. In the Los Angeles area alone the loss amounted to approximately 12,000 cattle and 8,000 hogs, including one of the most valuable Holstein herds in the United States. Nor do the losses mentioned take into account more than 4,000 unfinished, healthy cattle that were slaughtered and salvaged promptly as soon as the disease was discovered in the yards where they were being fed.

Prompt notification by telegraph or telephone.—Every moment's delay in notifying State and Government officials of a suspicious case, especially in any new outbreak of foot-and-mouth disease, is a hazard that may cost millions of dollars. In one case in California a telephone message to a stockyards would have headed off a consignment of exposed cattle which could readily have been diverted and salvaged by slaughter. Instead, a letter was written which was not received until after the cattle had been unloaded and had infected the public stockyards at Los Angeles.

In Texas, failure to adopt the speediest form of communication permitted one owner to cut out and throw on the range 51 stray cattle found on his ranch just 18 hours before his herd was found to be infected. These 51 stray cattle cost Texas in the neighborhood of $100,000, since every contact animal on the open range in that vicinity immediately became a potential spreader of the disease and had to be slaughtered. This not only extended suspicious territory, but prolonged the period of costly quarantine and embargoes against Texas.

Frequent and thorough inspections.—By making frequent and thorough inspections of all herds in the vicinity of infected premises, the disease was discovered in its first stages and the spread of the virus to other herds was reduced to a minimum.

Early slaughter and burial of diseased herds.—In those instances in which there was unavoidable delay in disposing of cattle on account of large numbers involved, inability to obtain trenching equipment quickly, and delay in excavating on account of hardpan and rock, there was frequently considerable spread of the infection to near-by herds. On the other hand, where diseased herds were buried or burned within 12 to 36 hours after infection appeared, there was little if any spread of the disease to other premises. Early slaughter is therefore essential in combating the spread of infection to other premises.

Optimism and confidence necessary.—In an atmosphere where owners are losing their means of livelihood, where children are seeing their pet lambs and calves shot down and buried in quicklime, and hired help is forced to look elsewhere for work, it ill becomes public officials and employees engaged in eradication work to show the slightest sign of pessimism. Yet in all outbreaks men on the side lines have publicly contended that eradication was impossible, that money was being spent to no possible advantage, and that the fight was lost before it was scarcely begun. They contended that flies, bumblebees, and baby chicks were important factors that were being ignored, that infected wild animals would carry the infection long distances, that quarantine, slaughter, and disinfection were unscientific, but on the other hand saltpeter and sulphur, salt, or other concoction would at once stop the disease as it had in the self-styled discoverer's home country. Frequently that country proved to be one where the infection was known to be firmly and permanently implanted.

All leaders in disease eradication should be optimistic, and they must also keep up the morale of the field forces, who are exposed to the whims and tirades of livestock owners and their friends, to strange and often scanty food, improvised beds, climatic changes, and other hardships, and who must wear their uncomfortable rubber outfits day after day from daylight to dark as they perform the drudgery necessary to their duties in the field.

Veterinarians and their professional duties.—Early in the California outbreak veterinarians not only performed their professional duties, but also shot the animals in the trenches, slashed the hides, and performed other work not of a veterinary character. Later, expert marksmen were employed and laborers did the slashing and cutting of the carcasses under supervision. This arrangement released more veterinarians to perform professional services in diagnosing diseases, in making inspections adjacent to infected premises, tracing rumors, addressing meetings, answering inquiries, and performing other duties of a related character. Of course, in emergency cases, veterinarians do some of the shooting and the work in the trench, but in order to conserve their services for professional work it should be the exception rather than the rule.

The quarantine, slaughter, and disinfection method.—With the present knowledge of foot-and-mouth disease, the quarantine, slaughter, and disinfection method is the most effective and economical way to combat outbreaks in the United States. Losses under this method, including indemnities, operating, and all other expenses, have not been so great in suppressing all the outbreaks in this country during the last 40 years as they would be in one year if the disease became established here and were fought by continental European quarantine and treatment methods.

Stringent quarantine of infected premises.—Efforts should be made to close completely all channels by which infection might escape from infected premises. No movement of livestock or commodities should be permitted from such premises. Dogs, cats, poultry, pigeons, etc., must be closely confined or killed.

Owners, their families, and hired help should be quarantined on the premises until after the cleaning and disinfection are completed. Guards should work under the direction of the inspector in charge and should be placed properly in order to enforce all quarantine measures strictly.

Unreasonable quarantines.—Unreasonable State quarantines and embargoes not based on experience or scientific knowledge of the disease, cause tremendous losses to the agricultural and commercial interests of States where infection is present and also to these interests in other parts of the country.

Organization of forces.—Consolidation of State and Federal forces under one directing head avoids duplication of work and conflict in eradication methods. It also fixes responsibility for the conduct of the work and the results.

ORGANIZATION OF THE
UNITED STATES DEPARTMENT OF AGRICULTURE

November 22, 1926

Secretary of Agriculture	W. M. JARDINE.
Assistant Secretary	R. W. DUNLAP.
Director of Scientific Work	A. F. WOODS.
Director of Regulatory Work	WALTER G. CAMPBELL.
Director of Extension Work	C. W. WARBURTON.
Director of Information	NELSON ANTRIM CRAWFORD.
Director of Personnel and Business Administration	W. W. STOCKBERGER.
Solicitor	R. W. WILLIAMS.
Weather Bureau	CHARLES F. MARVIN, *Chief.*
Bureau of Agricultural Economics	LLOYD S. TENNY, *Acting Chief.*
Bureau of Animal Industry	JOHN R. MOHLER, *Chief.*
Bureau of Plant Industry	WILLIAM A. TAYLOR, *Chief.*
Forest Service	W. B. GREELEY, *Chief.*
Bureau of Chemistry	C. A. BROWNE, *Chief.*
Bureau of Soils	MILTON WHITNEY, *Chief.*
Bureau of Entomology	L. O. HOWARD, *Chief.*
Bureau of Biological Survey	E. W. NELSON, *Chief.*
Bureau of Public Roads	THOMAS H. MACDONALD, *Chief.*
Bureau of Home Economics	LOUISE STANLEY, *Chief.*
Bureau of Dairy Industry	C. W. LARSON, *Chief.*
Office of Experiment Stations	E. W. ALLEN, *Chief.*
Office of Cooperative Extension Work	C. B. SMITH, *Chief.*
Library	CLARIBEL R. BARNETT, *Librarian.*
Federal Horticultural Board	C. L. MARLATT, *Chairman.*
Insecticide and Fungicide Board	J. K. HAYWOOD, *Chairman.*
Packers and Stockyards Administration	JOHN T. CAINE III, *in Charge.*
Grain Futures Administration	J. W. T. DUVEL, *in Charge.*

This circular is a contribution from

Bureau of Animal Industry	JOHN R. MOHLER, *Chief.*

83

CPSIA information can be obtained
at www.ICGtesting.com
Printed in the USA
BVHW041122150119
537879BV00009B/223/P

9 780266 834601